THREE
NEW PLAYS
FOR
YOUNG ACTORS

Also edited by Kerry Muir

Childsplay
A Collection of Scenes and Monologues for Childern

THREE NEW PLAYS FOR YOUNG ACTORS

From The Young Actor's Studio

Edited by Kerry Muir

PROMENADE *by Josh Adell*
SUMMER *by Gideon Brower*
BEFRIENDING BERTHA *by Kerry Muir*

LIMELIGHT EDITIONS
New York

First Limelight Edition   May 2001

Copyright © 2001 by Kerry Muir

See page xi for copyright and performance information on each of the plays included in this book.

All rights reserved under International and Pan-American Copyright Conventions. Published in the United States by Proscenium Publishers Inc., New York.

Manufactured in the United States of America.

Text design by Jeffrey H. Fitschen.

Library of Congress Cataloging in Publication Data

Three new plays for young actors : from the Young Actor's Studio / edited by Kerry Muir.
    p. cm.
    Contents: Promenade / by Josh Adell — Summer / by Gideon Brower — Befriending Bertha / by Kerry Muir.
    ISBN 0-87910-957-2
    1. Children's plays, American. [1. Plays.]   I. Muir, Kerry.   II. Muir, Kerry. Befriending Bertha.   III. Adell, Josh. Promenade.   IV. Brower, Gideon. Summer.   V. Young Actor's Studio.

PS625.5 .T53 2001
813'.540809282 — dc21

                                                        2001029123

For all the young actors
who brought these roles to life.

CONTENTS

ACKNOWLEDGEMENTS

This book would not have been possible without the help and support of Jacqueline Wolff, Jeff Alan-Lee and the gang at Class Act's Young Actor's Studio, David Brandt, Max and Lorna at The (beautiful) Ventura Court Theater in Studio City, Vaughn Armstrong, Jed Mills, Matt Howell, Megan Zakarian, Bettina Covo and Brian Taylor, John L. Bader, Chris Sena, Kris Jonson and Ead Daniels. The Writers and Actors Lab in Los Angeles, Jeff Endler, Michael Hiller — and all the kids who brought these words to life.

A special thanks to Charlie Dierkop, Claudette Sutherland, my family, and to Mel Zerman, Roxanna Font, Peter Cummins, and Jeff Fitschen at Limelight Editions and to Marieke Gaboury.

Photography Credits

All photos for PROMENADE on pages 2–95 were taken by Michael Hiller.

Photos for SUMMER on pages 99–130 were taken by Kris Jonson.

The cast photo for SUMMER on page 98 was taken by Kerry Muir.

All photos for BEFRIENDING BERTHA on pages 131–199 were taken by John L. Bader.

THANKS TO THE YOUNG ACTORS WHOSE PHOTOS APPEAR IN THIS BOOK:

Aubrey Brandt, Jenae Frye, Fay Gallagher, Cherylynn Glaser, Agnes Hewitt, Coleman Kelly, Lane Kozloff, Morgan Lewis, Hannah May, Gary Ohanian, Tommy Peterson, Jessica Rinsky, T.J. Ritchie, Tess Siedman, Andrew Shafer, Alison Shafer, Jaime Vazquez, Vlad Vizireanu and Galina Zhukhov.

PERMISSIONS FOR PERFORMANCE

ABOUT CLASS ACT'S YOUNG ACTOR'S STUDIO

The three plays that you are about to read were written by commissioned playwrights and/or faculty members of Class Act's Young Actor's Studio.

The Young Actor's Studio was founded in 1996 by its Artistic Director, Jeff Alan-Lee. Its faculty and commissioned playwrights, past and present, have included Josh Adell, Elizabeth Bauman, Gideon Brower, Casey Hendershot, Tim Mikulecky, Kerry Muir, Christopher Sena, Karen Tarleton and Megan Zakarian.

The goal of Class Act's Young Actor's Studio is to develop the young actor's craft. The studio is also dedicated to innovating new dramatic works made specifically for young actors. Students get the chance to originate new plays, and also to witness the writer's process on an interactive level and see how a playwright actually works. Class Act's Young Actor's Studio also encourages kids to write and develop their own work.

If you live in the Los Angeles area, and are interested in knowing more about Class Act's Young Actor's Studio, you can find out more information by looking on its web site: www.youngactorsstudio.com.

PROMENADE

SUMMER

BEFRIENDING BERTHA

ABOUT THE PLAYS

The following three plays provide an exciting range of roles for young actors to play:

Promenade takes William Shakespeare's *As You Like It* and re-sets it in a modern-day, public junior high school. When a young girl named Sammy finds herself without a date to the junior high school prom, she comes up with a wild plan. Like the heroine of *As You Like It*, she disguises herself as a boy in order to make friends with the guy she likes, in the hope that she can get him to ask her to the prom. But first, in order to pass herself off believably as a guy, she must take some acting lessons from the school's resident thespian, Francois. Not only does she learn about acting, but also about friendship, loyalty—and the importance of being true to oneself.

In *Summer*, a teenage girl named Alice looks back on the summer when she was only nine—a summer when she and her friends were bored and hot, and it seemed like nothing interesting ever happened to them. Back then, her biggest concern was coming up with a surefire way to win first place in the local talent show. It was also the summer that her older brother fell in love with romantic Italian movie plots and a girl named Gina; the summer her dreamy older sister taught herself how to ballroom dance from a tape. And looking back on a summer when supposedly "nothing" happened, Alice discovers that "nothing" was actually something after all.

In *Befriending Bertha*, three elementary school children who seem to have nothing in common—a boy who can't stop talking, a girl who can barely speak, and a flashy, mysterious girl who claims that she drives her own Cadillac—form an unlikely bond. Together they weave a web of fantasy and drama, inventing a magical reality in which they can seek refuge from their problems in ordinary life. When the children's world of fantasy collides with the adult world of reality, however, each child is faced with the challenge of finding a way to deal with the truth, and yet still keep hope alive.

And while each of these plays is unique, telling very different types of tales, they all share a common theme: kids have an inherent need for story, a really good story, even when (as in the play *Summer*) there seems to be no sign of a story in sight. The characters in these plays manufacture stories for all kinds of reasons: to cope with boredom, to handle a crisis—even to navigate the pitfalls of getting a date! They play with story, fantasy and make-believe in an effort to find answers and authenticity in their lives. Like actors, they try on roles. And that is why each of these plays contains so many rich roles for young actors to play—they get to play characters who, more often than not, are *themselves* playing characters.

Enjoy.

PROMENADE

by Josh Adell

- for Megan -

PROMENADE was written as a commissioned work for Class Act's Young Actor's Studio. It was directed by Jeff Alan-Lee and Kerry Muir and produced June 2000 at The Ventura Court Theater in Studio City with the following cast:

CAST

Tabatha Sue........................Tommy Peterson

Amanda Lou ....Cherylynn Glaser

Stanky.............................Cherylynn Glaser

Scabby............................. Tommy Peterson

Sammy...................................Hannah May

Daisy.................................. Jessica Rinsky

Roxanna ....Marina Michelson

Duane .... Lane Kozloff

Squirrel .... Vlad Vizireanu

Francois............................. Coleman Kelly

P R O L O G U E

In the dark we hear…

Tabatha Sue and Amanda Lou
(*With overwhelming spirit.*) GOOD MORNING,
PIRANHAS!!!!!!!!

A sharp pool of light bathes Tabatha Sue and Amanda Lou
who sit at a table and shout the morning announcements into
microphones. They wear school colors, blue and gold. They
are surrounded with blue and gold flags, ribbons, and flow-
ers. Their tag-team shtick is inexhaustibly enthusiastic.

Tabatha Sue
It's Friday, May 5th. I'm Tabatha Sue…

Amanda Lou
…and I'm Amanda Lou with your…

Tabatha Sue and Amanda Lou
…Public Junior High School Ultra Ultra Good
Morning Announcement!

Tabatha Sue
YOU KNOW WHAT IT'S TIME FOR, KIDS!

Amanda Lou
High flown hair-do's, diamond earrings, gold
cuff links…

Tabatha Sue
…clip-on bow ties, starchy shirts, smooooooth
close shaves…

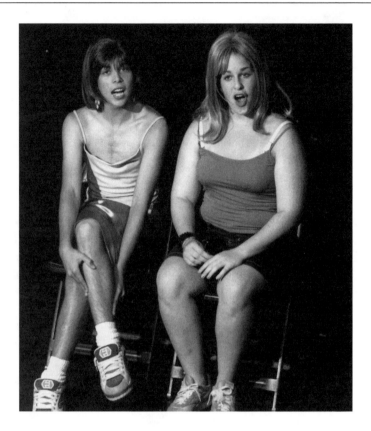

Amanda Lou
…excessive eye shadow, exciting cologne, glitter galore…

Tabatha Sure
…French manicures, fake lashes, fabulous flowers!

Amanda Lou
Ask what color is her dress!

Tabatha Sue
Don't stick him with the pin!

Amanda Lou
Pictures...

Tabatha Sue
Videos...

Amanda Lou
Pictures...

Tabatha Sue
Videos...

Amanda Lou
Pictures...

Tabatha Sue
Videos...

Amanda Lou
Teary mothers...

Tabatha Sue
...suspicious fathers...

Amanda Lou
...big brother chaperones...

Tabatha Sue and Amanda Lou
...limousiiiiiiiiiiines!!!

Amanda Lou
Jammin' DJ...

Tabatha Sue
...pumpin' speakers...

Amanda Lou
...dazzlin' disco...

Tabatha Sue
...sweaty dance floor...

Amanda Lou
....plenty of sloooooow songs...

Tabatha Sue
...extra concealer to hide the hickeys...

Amanda Lou
...the clock strikes twelve...

Tabatha Sue and Amanda Lou
...sweet dreams came true!

Pause.

Tabatha Sue
What does all this mean? You guessed it
Pirhanhas...

Tabatha Sue and Amanda Lou
...The Public Junior High School Prom!

Amanda Lou
Our last hurrah before we leave this safe pond
and swim into the dangerous waters of
American High.

Tabatha Sue and Amanda Lou
THE PROM!

Tabatha Sue
A celebration of our magnificence, our beauty and, of course, OUR FIERY PIRANHA SPIRIT!

Amanda Lou
Buy your prom tickets today! Only $99.99 for a single and $169.99 for a pair…

Tabatha Sue
…it pays to have a date.

Tabatha Sue and Amanda Lou
AND THAT'S THE SCOOP!

Tabatha Sue
I'm Tabatha Sue…

Amanda Lou
…and I'm Amanda Lou for…

Tabatha Sue and Amanda Lou
…Public Junior High.

Tabatha Sue
P.S. Principal Touchstone reminds us that even though the greatest weekend of our lives starts tomorrow — today is for learning.

Amanda Lou
So if you're caught out of class without a Piranha Pass our hall monitor Daniel "The Squirrel" Lowenstein will serve you with a…

Tabatha Sue
(*Making sounds of dramatic music.*) DA! DA! DA!

Amanda Lou
...detention! Have a positive...

Tabatha Sue
...perfect...

Amanda Lou
...peppy...

Tabatha Sue
...Pre-Prom...

Amanda Lou
...Piranha Day! PEACE!

Tabatha Sue
OUT!

A C T   1

A bell sounds. The lights jump from Tabatha Sue and Amanda Lou to the empty main hallway of Public Junior High. There are banners that read "Piranhas Rock", "Piranhas Roll" and "Piranhas Rule".

Enter Stanky, Scabby and Sammy. They are loud, rebellious chicks who dress in punk, funk and junk. Messy hair, torn plaid, ripped concert T-shirts, black boots, etc.

Stanky
The Prom can kiss my big ole' butt.

Scabby
The Prom can smell my cheesy toes.

Stanky
The Prom is a parade of gluttonous wealth!
All the snobs show off daddy's upper class
riches with their satins, velvets, laces, blah
blah blah! (*She makes a vomit sound.*)

Scabby
The Prom is a sexist extravaganza! Little girls sit
at home for weeks hoping just one guy will call.
"Oh please please please ask me so I can brag to
all my girlfriends who don't have a date."

Stanky
The Prom can sniff my arm pits.

Scabby
The Prom can KISS MY GRITS!

Sammy
RIGHT ON!

*They slam dance. Daisy enters, holding an enormous binder
that has papers sticking out every which way. She is Public
Junior High's yearbook editor, overly sentimental. She wears
flowers in her hair.*

Daisy
Hi Stanky, hi Scabby, hi Sammy. Can y'all
believe it's already Prom weekend? It seems
like yesterday we were terrified sixth graders
wandering slack-jawed through the halls of
Public. But we clung to each other through

thick and thin, sharing all our victories and
defeats with a special love. Ya'll, as yearbook
editor I've named this year's album OUR
TRUE HEARTS. It's almost finished, but I
need the perfect prom quotation. Can ya'll
share your feelings about our upcoming
weekend together?

Stanky spits in Daisy's face. Daisy calmly wipes it away.

Daisy (*cont'd*)
Ok. Maybe later I'll take some friendship
photos of ya'll?

Scabby

Daisy, is it true you paste posters of Principal Touchstone on the ceiling over your bed?

Daisy

Gross! No!

Scabby

That's what I wrote on the bathroom walls.

Daisy storms off. The chicks laugh.

Stanky

Chicks, give me your pinkies…pronto! (*All three girls link pinkies.*) We're the only real people in this mental institution, so from now on…especially next year in high school…let's vow to stick together.

Scabby

We'll stick together hard-core. And that includes, ladies, boycotting *boys* — - short-skirt-dreaming, cheerleader-loving, narrow-minded *boys*. We'll call ourselves the Ms. Fits!

Stanky

The Ms. Fits it is! As far as this comedy called the Prom goes, here's the plan: there's a bottle of vodka in my step-dad's liquor cabinet. Let's suck it down, sneak into the masquerade, 'cause I ain't got $99.99, and spike the punch bowl!

Scabby

RAD!

Sammy

What's it like to be drunk?

Stanky

You'll know tomorrow night. On the count of three, burp to seal our vow. ONE. TWO. THREE...

The chicks inhale. Just before they are able to burp, Stanky and Scabby FREEZE. Sammy approaches the audience.

Sammy

(*Aside.*) What am I doing? Is this who I really am? If I show any doubt, these chicks'll spit in *my* face. But a bottle of vodka? This is not who I want to be...

The FREEZE is broken and all three chicks burp onto their hands.

Stanky

The vow is sealed. NEVER TO BE BROKEN. NEVER.

There is a noise stage left.

Sammy

Someone's coming!

Scabby

Squirrel the Pest.

Sammy

One more detention and I'm suspended.

Stanky

Scatter!

Stanky and Scabby exit. Sammy follows, but then she sees Duane, the school hunk, about to enter. Transfixed, she finds a hiding place from which she can watch him.

Duane enters, fighting with Roxanna. Roxanna wears the most expensive clothes in school. Her hair and make-up are perfect. Duane wears a blue and gold letter jacket.

Sammy watches them from her hiding place.

Roxanna
You told me we were getting a limousine!

Duane
But Roxanna, wouldn't it be funner if my sister drove us in the Taurus?

Roxanna
What are you saying to me? I have a crystal clear image of me stepping out of a black limousine. You promised me, Duane.

Duane
It's not that we're *not* getting a…it's just that…I mean the Taurus is a dark navy station wagon…

Roxanna
I AM THE PROM QUEEN! Do you know what happens to 90% of the Public Junior High Prom Queens? By sophmore year of high school they're forgotten. They don't make Varsity cheerleader, or even mascot, so they end up as one of a hundred girls in the pathetic pep squad! Sweetie, this Prom is my fifteen minutes. My crowning achievement. My peak. It must be the greatest night of my life…because it's the only night I have!

Tabatha Sue and Amanda Lou enter skipping and singing with unbridled joy!

Tabatha Sue and Amanda Lou
34! 34! 34 HOURS! 34 HOURS 'TIL PROM!

RIGHT ON! *WE'RE THE BOMB!* 34 HOURS
'TIL PROM!

They exit skipping!

Roxanna
Please, Duane. Let me have my glory before it
all ends. You told me you liked me.

Duane
I totally totally totally totally like you.

Roxanna
Well, then?

Duane
I spent all my money on wine coolers.

Roxanna
Come again?

Duane
I bought eight cases of wine coolers. But I had
to pay my sister's boyfriend who has a fake
license two hundred bucks to get them. I
wanted to surprise you.

Roxanna
Who on earth drinks eight cases of wine coolers?

Duane
My sister loves 'em. They're fruity.

Roxanna
You are so dumb! You are so dumb! You are

so dumb!

Duane
Don't you totally totally totally like me?

Daisy enters with her binder.

Daisy
Oh my God, ya'll! The Prom King and Queen!
Give me an ever-lasting reflection on a night
you'll remember for the rest of your life.

Roxanna
(*Right in Daisy's face.*)
AAAAAAAAAHHHHHHHHGGGGGGG!!!

Daisy exits.

Duane
Hey. That's mean.

Roxanna
I'll be the first Prom Queen in the history of
Public to step out of a *station wagon*! NO! If I
don't pull up to the red carpet in a beautiful
black stretch limousine, then I'm not going to
the Prom at all.

Duane
THEN HAVE A SWELL TIME AT HOME
ALONE, ROXANNA!

Roxanna
I WILL, YOU DUMB JOCK!

Roxanna furiously exits. Pause. Duane sobs. Sammy quiet-
ly enters from her hiding place. She observes Duane sobbing.
In mid-sob Duane FREEZES.

Sammy
(*Aside.*) Whoa. Duane the Hunk in
tears…without a date to the Prom. Poor boy. I
would never demand a limousine. I'd be a
perfect date. Imagine, *me* going to the Prom
with Duane the Hunk…Captain of the
wrestling team. Imagine me in a white satin
dress, with white shoes and a white rose
corsage that Duane slides around my wrist,
goose bumps shooting up my arm. Imagine me
pulling up to a red carpet, stepping out of a
navy Taurus station wagon with Duane the
Hunk on one arm and goose bumps on the
other. *That's* who I want to be! But he would
ask a wart to the ball before me. I'LL ASK HIM!
But stupid custom says girls can't ask boys to
the Prom. I'll look like a bigger freak than I
already am. Plus the Ms. Fits would have a
field day hazing my face. Why am I so
powerless? Ohhhhhhh, who cares how I look?
I'll be the first girl to wrestle custom and pin him
to the mat! I'll win my rose corsage, my red
carpet, my navy Taurus. I'll ask The Hunk to the
Prom right now! And so begins the new me!

Duane's FREEZE is broken and he continues to cry as before.
Sammy confidently approaches him.

Sammy (*cont'd*)
Duane. (*Duane turns and stares at her. She*

suddenly gets very nervous.) Uh…uh…ha ha….
Will you go…? Hee hee…. Do you wanna…?
Uh…uh…hee hee….

Duane sobs again and exits.

Sammy (cont'd)
I'm nobody. Powerless. Nobody.

Squirrel, the hall monitor, enters. He wears a badge. He's a small geek.

Squirrel
Do you have a Piranha Pass, Samantha?

Sammy
Squirrel! If I get another detention I'm suspended.

Squirrel
If you *skip* another detention you're suspended.

Sammy
Same thing, you hoser!

Squirrel
You used to be such a sweet girl, Samantha. What happened?

Sammy
The sweet girl thing didn't work. No one noticed.

Squirrel
We were friends. Now look at you.

Sammy

Well, look at *you*. You think you're the county sheriff. Do you like yourself?

Squirrel

I'm encouraging kids to stay in class. I'm performing a critical service for our feeble school system. (*Pause.*) You know my IQ is now 130?

Sammy

Woop dee doo.

Daisy enters trying to open a pill bottle.

Daisy

(*To herself.*) Uhhhgggg, child-proof Prozac!

Daisy stops, caught.

Daisy (*cont'd*)

Oh.

Squirrel

Daisy, you should be in Online Technology class.

Daisy

I'm starving for a quotation about the Prom for OUR TRUE HEARTS. I came out here to get your meaningful insights.

Squirrel

(*Writing on his detention pad.*) Hmm, let's see... "I know many pasty bookworms in private schools who spout that the Prom is just frivolous play time, but actually valuable life lessons lie in public school social adventures. Adolescents must make serious choices regarding friends, lovers, themselves. My informal hypothesis states that the Prom, the grandest affair of all, is just as meaningful to education as the library." How's that for a quote?

Daisy
I was looking for something a little more like, "The Prom is totally special to my heart."

Squirrel
Here's your detention. Be in The Hole at 3:30.

Daisy
My first detention! Thanks for the memories, you pest.

Daisy exits, frustrated.

Sammy
You've successfully alienated yourself from every kid in this building.

Squirrel
I got accepted to Harvard. They want me to skip high school and begin next year. I'm the youngest accepted pre-med student in twenty years.

Sammy
(*Surprised.*) Congratulations.

Squirrel
Will you go to the Prom with me?

Sammy
What?

Squirrel

Don't you miss me, Samantha? After the
dance we could eat at The Magic Time
Machine, like we did for my 10th birthday.

Squirrel FREEZES.

Sammy

(*Aside.*) I got asked! I'm not a freak! I'm a
pretty girl with a date, who won't have to suck
down a bottle of vodka 'cause I'm lonely. I'll
accept —- and request a rose corsage.

*Sammy begins to answer Squirrel but then changes
her mind.*

Sammy *(cont'd)*

But this is *Squirrel*. Sure we had a blast at The
Magic Time Machine, but how will I look if I
go to the Prom with The Pest, who's sentenced
everyone to The Hole at least twice? He's no
Duane the Hunk.

She turns to Squirrel whose FREEZE is broken.

Squirrel

What do ya say, Samantha?

Sammy

Sorry, Squirrel.

Squirrel

Who do you think you are, "Sammy"? Drop
the attitude!

Sammy
The Prom can kiss my big ole butt! It's flaky! And so are you for wanting to go!

Squirrel
Fine! (*Shoving a detention slip into her hands.*) If you're not in The Hole at three-thirty, Principal Touchstone will suspend you. Now get back to your Web Design class!

Sammy
Kiss off, Pest.

Sammy takes the detention and charges off.

Squirrel
(*Aside.*) Why is she playing the punk? Her clothes, her words, her hate…all counterfeit. She's heading down a lonely road. I must save our friendship, and more vitally, save her from herself. But I've read that if you try to rescue a psychologically disturbed person, they reject you. So I'll turn the tables and force her to rescue *me*. But how?

Duane enters, crying softly.

Squirrel (*cont'd*)
Piranha Pass, Duane?

No answer. Squirrel writes out a detention.

Squirrel (*cont'd*)
I'll see you in The Hole this afternoon. Three-thirty sharp.

*Duane grabs Squirrel by the shirt lapels and slams him
against the lockers.*

Duane
You Pest! Can't you see I'm crying?!

Squirrel
You need to cry *in class.*

Duane
AAAAAAAAHHHHHHHHHGGGGGGGG!

Duane pulls his arm back to slug Squirrel, then FREEZES.

Squirrel
(*Aside.*) THAT'S IT! I'll have Duane pulverize
my face *in detention.* Samantha will see me
lying on the floor, and run to my rescue. As
she's kneeling by my side, I'll dramatically
whisper, "Won't you go to the Prom with me?"
She'll caress my face and reply, "Yes, Squirrel,
yes." And in slow motion, she'll lightly kiss
my lips. You see why I have a 130 IQ?
Because I'm a genius.

Squirrel turns to Duane. Duane's FREEZE is broken.

Duane
...AAAAAAAAAAHHHHHHHHGGGGGG!

Squirrel
STOP!

Duane stops.

Duane
What?

Squirrel
I'll pay you three hundred and fifty dollars to
postpone this pounding until detention.

Duane
Why?

Squirrel
I want to impress a girl! Pity works, my friend
—pity works.

Duane
No way, Pest. Principal Touchstone will
expel my face. (*He begins to punch again.*)
AAAHHGGG!

Squirrel
HALT! I'll arrange it so he won't be there.
I'm supposed to oversee the Prom decoration
committee after school. But I'll have him do
that while I monitor The Hole.

Duane
He'll never go for that!

Squirrel
Yes! He wants to decorate. He loves to suck
helium from balloons.

Squirrel FREEZES.

Duane

(*Aside.*) Hey, I can get a black limousine with that kind of cash. And win Roxanna back. What good is eight cases of wine coolers if you have no one to share them with?

Duane looks at Squirrel. Squirrel's FREEZE is broken.

Duane *(cont'd)*
Four hundred dollars. Cash.

Squirrel
Deal! (*He fishes in his pocket and pulls out a ton of cash.*) If you hit me before Samantha arrives that's a breach of contract and I get a refund.

Duane
Where'd you get all that scratch?

Squirrel
Kids will pay pretty to avoid The Hole. I'm not proud of it, but we all have our dark side. Now here's the scenario this afternoon: you're furious that you have detention, and when I politely ask you to relax, you irrationally go crazy and slug me. You're perfect for the role.

Duane
Anything you say.

Squirrel gives him the cash and a detention slip.

Squirrel
I look forward to my beating.

Duane
Me, too.

They shake hands.

Squirrel
Now get back to International E-Commerce
and study hard!

Duane
(*Thrilled.*) OK!

Duane and Squirrel exit. Sammy enters.

Sammy
(*Aside.*) I can't stop dreaming of Duane the
Hunk. What can I do? What's the use of high
school if it's a more inflated version of junior
high? Five times the socials, five times the
hunks, five times the bottles of vodka.

Tabatha Sue and Amanda Lou enter dancing!

Tabatha Sue and Amanda Lou
33! 33! 33 HOURS! 33 HOURS TILL PROM!
PEACE MON! PEACE MON! DANCIN'
LIKE A RASTA MON! 33 HOURS TILL
PROM!

They exit dancing!

Sammy
(*Aside.*) How lucky is Squirrel who gets to go
to Harvard next year and skip the waste of
American High.

*Francois enters, wearing a black turtleneck. He puts up
posters that read "William Shakespeare's 'As You Like It'
starring Francois Fisher. Saturday, May 6th. Call 981-1746
for details." Sammy watches him.*

Sammy (cont'd)
Be careful, Francois! The Pest is foaming at the
mouth giving detentions.

Francois
You give good counsel, friend.

Sammy
Huh?

Francois
Samantha, you're not going to the Prom, are
you?

Sammy
The Prom can smell my cheesy toes.

Francois
Brilliant! Come to my one man show of
Shakespeare's *As You Like It*. I'm mounting his
twenty-ninth play in its entirety, in my garage,
on Prom night.

Sammy
Seriously?

Francois
Seriously! *As You Like It* is a brilliant comedy!
A passionate woman named Rosalind falls in
love with a handsome young wrestler. When
she's unexpectedly forced to flee her home, she
dresses like a man to protect herself from any
danger in the woods. By chance, she
encounters the handsome young wrestler
and — still disguised as a man — she teaches the

wrestler to love her true self…as a woman.
I'm playing all the characters, running the
lights and performing live music.

Sammy

(*Aside.*) "Disguised as a man she teaches the
wrestler how to love her true self…as a
woman!" Now there's something to do! Dare I?

Sammy turns back to Francois.

Sammy (*cont'd*)

You dress as a woman?

Francois

I dress as a woman dressing as a man!

Sammy

How believable is your woman dressed as a
man?

Francois

EVERY CHARACTER I PORTRAY, MAN
OR WOMAN, IS AS BELIEVABLE AS
BELIEVABILITY ITSELF!

Sammy

Would you believe this: I want to disguise
myself as a man to teach a handsome young
wrestler how to ask me to the Prom!

Francois

Unbelievable.

Sammy

I know.

Tabatha Sue and Amanda Lou enter skipping and giggling!

Tabatha Sue and Amanda Lou
32 HOURS 58 MINUTES! 32 HOURS 58
MINUTES! 32 HOURS...

Tabatha Sue and Amanda Lou exit!

Sammy
Please help me, Francois. I need some
confidence to talk with Duane. I need to act
like someone else — like someone brave. I
don't know what else to do, and time's
wasting. What do ya say?

Francois
I'd say it's the most brilliant directorial
challenge I've ever met! Your man will be
honest, real and believe you me...most
believable. Let's make haste to the theatre to
find a suitable suit to suit your potential...
suit-uation.

Sammy
Huh?

Francois
Let's hurry and get a costume.

Francois grabs her hand and they exit. Roxanna enters.

Roxanna
(*Aside.*) Did I do the right thing? What's
worse, staying home on Prom night or being
seen in a Ford? People don't realize the

responsibility a Prom Queen faces. It's
imperative that I'm radiant, beautiful, perfect.
That's the Prom Queen custom — and burden.
If I break tradition they'll ridicule me forever.
I'd rather stay home.

Stanky and Scabby enter.

Stanky
Miss Roxanna, heard you dumped the Hunk
'cause your head wants to be seen in a limo.

Roxanna
So what?

Stanky
Wanna pretend you're a big star?

Scabby
Here's an idea...go to the Prom with *us*. We'll
get you a limo.

Roxanna
Gross!

Stanky
You'll get everyone's attention! Hang out with
some risky chicks like us. You'll be
remembered forever.

Scabby
I can't wait to spread the news! Especially to
Seniors at American High!

Daisy enters, sees the three girls.

Daisy

OH CRAP! Wait a minute, I'll save you the trouble... (*She spits all over her notebook and herself.*) Happy?!?

Daisy exits.

Scabby

All you Prom Queens make me sick. God gave you great hair, a sweet bod, the hottest stud in school...and you want a limo, too.

Stanky

The price of a limo can feed a starving kid in Armenia for a whole year, you self-centered snob! I hope you rot down below with all the other Prom Queens!

Squirrel enters.

Squirrel

Ladies, why don't you finish this enlightening conversation in The Hole this afternoon.

He hands then each a detention slip and exits.

Roxanna

Thanks a lot, dogs!

Stanky and Scabby exit, laughing.

Roxanna (*cont'd*)

(*Aside.*) Detention! It's scandalous. But those stinky chicks are right. I'm lucky to have the

hunkiest guy in school. And I'll never be
lonely 'cause I'm so hot. I guess the right
thing to do is enjoy being with people whether
I'm the Prom Queen or a peon in the pep
squad. The limos in life are only rentals — the
friendships you *own*. But I'm afraid I've lost
Duane forever. (*Pause.*) I'll win him back. I
won't ask him to the Prom, though — I've got
to get him to re-ask me. How? I'll act like a
good person — sweet, caring and selfless. I'll
completely transform myself. I'll wear a pink
bow in my hair, a pretty little sweater and
flats. Oh, gross…flats. Well, a girl's gotta do
what a girl's gotta do. The King and Queen
will go to the Prom again — no matter what
the cost!

Roxanna exits. Francois enters alone. He looks around.

Francois
Ok. The coast is clear.

*Sammy enters dressed as a guy. She wears a backwards base-
ball cap, an oversized flannel shirt and a fake goatee. She
looks terrified.*

Sammy
I don't know about this, Francois. Let's go
back to the theatre.

Francois
I highly doubt we'll find our wrestler in the
theatre.

Sammy
No one will buy this costume.

Francois
You must *become* the part. Now, the most important trait of every man is his handshake! A shake must be kind, yet powerful. It must say, "I'm your friend, yet I can beat you in a fight." Let's fly to't.

Sammy
What?

Francois
Offer me your hand.

Sammy
Oh.

Sammy offers Francois her hand.

Francois
I don't want to kiss your hand, I want to shake it. Try it again like a *man.*

Sammy offers Francois her hand. They shake.

Francois *(cont'd)*
Firmer. (*Sammy squeezes harder.*) Firmer. (*Sammy squeezes harder.*) Put some ego into it. Imagine you're shaking Roxanna's hand. (*Sammy squeezes harder.*) Ow ow ow ow ow. Okay, got it. Good. Not so hard.

Sammy
Are you okay?

Francois
Oh yeah. Very committed work. You're a very enthusiastic man.

Sammy
Come on, someone's gonna catch us out here!

Francois

Balderdash! Now your voice. A deep, low, resonant sound from your diaphram.

Sammy

(*Low voice.*) Yo, Francois, my boy. How 'bout you an me hit the mall yo and hook up some pretty young thangs in tiny skirts?

Francois

Astonishing! And strut a little.

Sammy

(*Strutting.*) Yo yo, Francois, I want all the rich chicks so bad, man. I love them so much!

Francois

YES! Grunt more.

Sammy

I'm dyin' for babes, man! I'm a guy and all I want are babes!

Francois

Don't be afraid of a butt scratch every once in a while.

Sammy

(*Low, grunting voice, strutting, scratching butt.*) Babes babes babes babes babes babes babes babes babes babes babes!

Francois

YOU'RE A TRIUMPH!

Sammy
Shhhhh.

Francois
Shhhhh.

Sammy
You really think?

Francois
Samantha, you must risk everything you have! Life is not a dress rehearsal!

Sammy
(*Low voice.*) You're right. (*Pause.*) Yo, Francois, man to man: how come you didn't date up a sweet honey for the dance?

Francois
Ask a fair maiden to accompany me to the revels? I've been preparing *As You Like It* for months. Tomorrow night is the only night to open.

Sammy
(*Low voice.*) But don't you get, like, lonely working on the play all by yourself in your garage?

Francois
Man to man: yes. There aren't any ladies who fancy the idea of dating me. I'm miscast in a production like the Promenade. But when I enter the world of a play, and become anyone I want to be, nothing else in the world matters. I feel useful, alive, whole. I feel like a man.

Sammy
I'm jealous.

Francois
When the play is over, desolation takes the stage.

Sammy
At least you feel useful for a little bit.

Francois
A little bit.

Duane enters, counting money.

Sammy
Duane!

Duane
AAAAHHHH! You scared me — -dude.

Francois
(*Obviously acting.*) I'll see you later, my man.

Sammy
(*Forgetting her low voice.*) Going so soon?

Francois clears his throat and grunts, reminding Sammy to become the part.

Sammy (*cont'd*)
Yo yo going so soon?

Francois
I'm desperately needed in the theatre! To your business, good Sir. And break a leg.

Sammy
Break a leg?!

Francois
It means good luck!

Francois exits part-way, then hides around the corner to watch. Duane crosses to exit but Sammy stops him.

Sammy/Guy
Yo, Duane, my boy.

Sammy extends her hand like a man. Duane takes it.

Duane
Ow ow ow ow ow.

Sammy/Guy

Oh, sorry. You okay?

Duane

Look out. I'm going to make up with my girlfriend before some other jock invites her to the Prom.

Sammy/Guy

Slow down, man. What are you, totally insane?

Duane

I got four hundred bucks to rent the limo she wanted.

Sammy/Guy

I can't believe what I'm hearing. Did it ever occur to you that she doesn't care about you? She's a high and mighty selfish Queen.

Duane

Do I know you?

Sammy/Guy

She's using your jockness to make herself look better. She gives us women a bad name.

Duane

Us women?

Sammy/Guy

(*Caught; thinking.*) Us women. Us women. That's…what…all the *chicks* say, man. (*She imitates a girl's voice.*) "Roxanna gives us women a bad name." She doesn't like you for who you really are. You're like a human trophy.

Duane
She doesn't like me for who I am?

Sammy/Guy
I'll give you some manly advice. I happen to
know a lovable girl named Samantha who is
dying for you to ask her to the Prom. She
cares about *you*, not the frills. Besides, you
could really teach the Queen a lesson if you
ask Sammy — I mean Samantha.

Duane
Samantha. Hmmm. I can't place her. (*Pause.*)
That little scruffy girl?

Sammy/Guy
(*Girl voice.*) SCRUFFY! WHO YOU CALLING
SCRUFFY YOU DUMB JOCK!

Duane
Wait a minute. What's wrong with this
picture? You must think I'm really stupid!

Sammy/Guy
I do?

Duane
What is this? Some kind of joke? Oh, my God,
are you for real?

Sammy/Guy
Oh…Duane, listen…

Duane
I'm not the dumb jock everyone says I am. I
got you figured out!

Sammy/Guy
(*About to take off her hat.*) ...I'm sorry...

Duane
You're gonna ask Roxanna to the Prom!

Sammy/Guy
Huh?

Duane
You wanna convince me she's a witch so I won't like her, then you'll mosey in and make your move. Pretty sneaky, man.

Sammy/Guy
Oh. Oh. Oh. Duane, you got it all wrong. (*Laughing nervously.*) Believe me, Roxanna is the last person in the world I would take to the Prom.

Duane
You're a liar. Get outta my way.

Sammy/Guy
Wait! (*Pause.*) Duane, I'm in love with...Samantha.

Duane
You're in love with Samantha?

Sammy/Guy
Yes, Duane, I'm in love with Samantha.

Duane
Then *you* ask her to the Prom.

Sammy/Guy

I would if I could, Duane, I would if I could.
You see, Samantha's always been a nobody, the
kind of Miss who gets the "dis'" from foxy
guys like you. But she's a real girl, with a real
heart. She's Public Junior High's Cinderella
and her fairy tale fantasy is you. She stays up
nights dreaming of your smile as you gently
take her hand, guiding her to the floor for the
last slow dance. (*Sammy begins to cry.*)
Because I love her so much, I want what she
wants. And she wants, more than anything in
the world, to be your Prom date.

Duane

(*Beginning to cry.*) Oh, little dude, don't cry. I
hate to see people cry. It always kills me.

Sammy/Guy
I'm sorry, I can't help it.

Duane
Neither can I.

Sammy/Guy
But you can, Duane. You can! Ask Sammy to the Prom, for me.

Duane
You're so noble, yet sensitive. You break my heart. (*Pause. Still crying:*) But Roxanna's a babe.

Sammy/Guy
Duane, be a man! Ask Samantha in the name of love!

Duane
In the name of love! You're right! I'll ask Samantha to the Prom!

Sammy/Guy
YOU WILL!?!

Duane
I will for you, dude. I will for you.

Sammy/Guy
YOU DON'T KNOW HOW MUCH THIS MEANS TO ME!

Duane
When should I ask her?

> **Sammy/Guy**
> After school!

> **Duane**
> I have detention!

> **Sammy/Guy**
> (*Thrilled.*) SHE DOES, TOO!!!

> **Duane**
> I'LL ASK HER THERE!!!

> **Sammy/Guy**
> I CAN'T WAIT!

> **Duane**
> (*Extending his hand.*) You're one of the best men I know!

> **Sammy/Guy**
> (*Shaking his hand.*) Thank you, my brother! Thank you!

> **Duane**
> Ow ow ow ow ow.

> **Sammy/Guy**
> Sorry, man.

Duane exits.

> **Sammy/Guy (*cont'd*)**
> (*Aside.*) I'm going to the Prom with Duane the Hunk! I'm a real girl with a real date! I'M SOMEBODY!

Sammy skips off like Tabatha Sue and Amanda Lou. Francois enters from his hiding place.

Francois

She's brilliant.

Lights fade. End of Act I.

A C T   I I

Lights up on Tabatha Sue and Amanda Lou in all their spirit, behind their microphones.

Tabatha Sue and Amanda Lou
HEEEEEYYYYYY PIRANHAS!

Tabatha Sue
Our last official school day before the ball has come to a close.

Amanda Lou
Congratulations!

Tabatha Sue
But before you run to the tanning salons…

Amanda Lou
…Principal Touchstone reminds you naughty children with detentions, Prom weekend does not exempt you from paying retribution for your evil sins.

Tabatha Sue
And now an advertisement from The Public Junior High Computer Club:

Amanda Lou
"Still dateless to the Prom? Too embarrassed to go stag?…

Tabatha Sue
...Then purchase the PJH Computer Club's Virtual Prom CD Rom!

Amanda Lou
Experience the Prom of your fantasies with one easy click of the mouse!

Tabatha Sue
Design your own date!...

Amanda Lou
...Tall, dark and handsome? Bodacious and ditzy?

Tabatha Sue
Decide your dinner...

Amanda Lou
...Caviar at The Russian Tea Room? Or some sloppy USDA prime at ol' Fatburger?

Tabatha Sue
Don't like dorky DJ's at dances?

Amanda Lou
Score your own soundtrack! There are over one hundred and fifty versions of *Shout!*... play them all! It's your Prom!

Tabatha Sue
With the PJH Computer Club's Virtual Prom CD Rom, no one has to feel alone!

Amanda Lou
On sale now in the computer lab for $289.95…

Tabatha Sue
…Better hurry, there's only three left!"

Tabtha Sue and Amanda Lou
AND THAT'S THE SCOOP!

Tabatha Sue
I'm Tabatha Sue…

Amanda Lou
…and I'm Amanda Lou for…

Tabatha Sue and Amanda Lou
…Public Junior High!

Amanda Lou
PEACE!

Tabatha Sue
OUT!

Lights up on The Hole. It looks like a holding pen in a downtown jail. There is a cold cement floor, a bunch of chairs, and a metal desk. A sign in red letters reads "YOU ARE BAD CHILDREN."

Sammy enters hastily. She nervously pulls out a compact mirror and tries to fix her messy hair. She practices saying "Yes".

Sammy

Yes. Oh…sure. Duane, I'm so surprised. I'd love to, Duane. Me, really?

Stanky and Scabby enter.

Stanky

SWEET! SAMMY IN THE HOLE!

Scabby

OH YEAH, BABY! MS. FITS IN THE HOLE!

Stanky and Scabby

YEAH!!!!!

Stanky and Scabby FREEZE.

Sammy

(*Aside.*) I'm so stupid! I should have known they'd get detention! If they see me being popular with Duane and breaking our vodka vow, they'll turn vile. I'll act too cool and throw them. Have courage, Samantha, you've come this far.

Stanky and Scabby's FREEZE is broken.

Stanky and Scabby

SAMMY! SAMMY! SAMMY! SAMMY! SAMMY! SAMMY!

Sammy

(*Unenthused.*) Oh, it's you…hey.

Stanky
Check this out, Sammy. We're gonna bring a camera to the costume party and once we've spiked the punch, we'll shoot pictures of prudes puking their pastries on their petticoats.

Scabby
And send the pictures to Seniors at American High.

Sammy
(*Uncaring.*) Whatever.

Stanky
Whatever?

Sammy
Whatever.

Stanky
What's your problem?

Sammy
You guys have the problem. Maybe you should get a life and lay off the Prom.

Scabby
What?!?

Sammy
Maybe the Prom isn't so bad.

Stanky
Yeah, it's great if you're daddy's named Warbucks and you're an arrogant show-off!

Scabby

The Prom's great if you wanna hop on the victim bandwagon and wait and pray and die to get asked.

Sammy

Maybe I don't have to wait and pray and die.

Stanky

What?

Sammy

Maybe I'm gonna get asked.

Stanky

No!

Scabby

You're breaking the boy boycott!

Daisy enters. She has dark circles under her eyes and her hair is a mess.

Daisy

Is this where I'm supposed to go for... (*She sees the punks.*) OH GREAT GOD IS THERE NO SALVATION?!?

Stanky

Oh, you're gonna get it today. I'll give you something to remember forever!

Stanky begins to spit, but Sammy intervenes.

Sammy

You want a perfect quotation for the yearbook,
Daisy?

Daisy

NO! PLEASE! I CAN'T TAKE IT! I JUST
CAN'T TAKE IT ANYMORE!

Sammy

How 'bout this: "The PJH Prom is special for
students because it's really about hanging with
friends, feeling beautiful inside and finding
your true self. The Prom is totally special to
my heart." I'm not gonna haze you anymore,
Daisy. I'm growing up.

Daisy

Oh, Sammy. That's perfect! (*Aside.*) Junior High isn't a cynical wasteland after all! (*She pulls a flower from her tangled hair and places it in Sammy's hair.*) Thank you! Thank you! Thank you!

Daisy and Sammy FREEZE.

Stanky

(*Aside.*) Who does she think she is? We promised to stick together. Does growing up mean ignoring your friends?

Scabby

(*Aside.*)   Could not even one skinny, zit-faced geek find it in his small heart to ask me to the Prom? Some feminist I am. I wish I had the spine to ask a guy myself.

Stanky and Scabby address each other.

Scabby (*cont'd*)

I guess the cool thing to do is act like we don't care about Sammy...

Stanky

Maybe we'll feel better if we haze the crap out of her.

Scabby

Good idea.

Daisy and Sammy's FREEZE is broken.

Daisy

Oh, Sammy, I have a great feel-good photo of
you for the "Friends" section of OUR TRUE
HEARTS. Let me find it.

*Daisy fishes in her huge binder for the picture. Stanky and
Scabby surround Sammy.*

Scabby

You broke our vow. Didn't know you were so
two-faced, Sammy.

Stanky

I guess you're just another princess hungry for
abuse.

Squirrel enters.

Squirrel

Have a seat, delinquents. This isn't social
hour. You need to be thinking of all the
important classroom education you missed
today.

Stanky and Scabby boo and hiss Squirrel.

Scabby

Where's Touchstone, you pesky chump?

Squirrel

He's decorating. The principal wanted to
supervise the helium tank again, so he
employed yours truly to monitor The Hole.
But don't think you can get away with any
foolery.

> ### Stanky
> You're a proud rodent, aren't ya?

> ### Squirrel
> Hey, Sammy, betcha anything by the end of
> detention you'll be goin' to the Prom with me.

> ### Sammy
> Hey, Squirrel, betcha you're *half* right.

Duane enters.

> ### Duane
> There a chick named Samantha here?

Squirrel walks directly to Duane.

> ### Squirrel
> Duane, I'm asking you in a very polite tone of
> voice to please take a seat.

*Squirrel closes his eyes and waits for Duane's punch, but
Duane walks past Squirrel and heads straight for Sammy.
He sits next to her.*

> ### Duane
> Is your name Samantha?

> ### Sammy
> (*Shy.*) Yes.

> ### Duane
> Funny, I never really noticed you before.

Sammy

Funny.

Duane

But for some reason, I feel like I know you.

Sammy

Ha...funny.

Duane

You know the Prom's tomorrow night.

Sammy

(*Casual.*) Oh, yeah...that's right...I heard something about that...

Duane

I'm not taking Roxanna. She doesn't like me for who I am.

Sammy

Oh...that's horrible.

Duane

Yeah, my heart is broken.

Sammy

You poor thing.

Stanky and Scabby watch in amazement as Sammy and Duane woo each other.

Squirrel

(*Aside.*) What is this flirtation? I have to make him belt me ASAP!

Squirrel approaches Duane and Sammy.

Squirrel (*cont'd*)
Excuse me, please! I am very kindly telling
you that talking is not allowed in The Hole,
Duane.

*Squirrel closes his eye again bracing himself for Duane's
punch, but again Duane ignores him.*

Duane
(*To Sammy.*) So, I heard that you don't have a
date to the Prom.

Sammy
Uh...I guess...

Duane
You're sweet.

Sammy
(*Batting her eyelashes.*) Thanks.

Squirrel
Duane, stop talking or I'll tell Principal
Touchstone.

Daisy, in happy oblivion, continues looking for Sammy's photo.

Daisy
Sammy, that friendship photo is in here
somewhere.

Everyone ignores Daisy.

Duane
(*To Sammy.*) I was wondering…

Sammy
Yes…?

Duane
If maybe you weren't doing anything
tomorrow…

Sammy
Yes…?

Duane
Maybe…uh…maybe…uh…

Sammy
Yes…?

Squirrel
DO NOT SPEAK ANOTHER WORD,
DUANE!

Duane
(*Still to Sammy.*) …maybe we could, you know,
if you want, we could go to the Pr—

Roxanna enters.

Roxanna
Duane!

*Duane looks up to see Roxanna wearing a cute pink bow in
her hair, a pretty sweater and – of course – flats.*

Duane
Roxanna. What are you doing in The Hole?

Roxanna
I sacrificed my perfect attendance record just
to see you one last time before the weekend.

Sammy
Duane, you were saying…?

Duane is mesmerized by the "new" Roxanna.

Duane
Roxanna, you look so…

Roxanna
Soft and sweet?

Duane
Yeah.

Sammy
Duane…

Roxanna
(*Still to Duane, ignoring Sammy.*) Speaking of
this weekend…I'm really concerned for you. I
want to make sure you're going to be all right
tomorrow night.

*Duane walks to Roxanna leaving Sammy behind. Squirrel
follows Duane tapping him on the shoulder.*

Duane
You're concerned for me?

Roxanna

Are you going to be able to survive tomorrow night?

Duane

(*Pouting.*) I don't know.

Sammy

Duane, you were about to ask me something...

Sammy tries to go to Duane, but Stanky blocks her way.

Stanky

Sammy! Going for the gold, huh?

Scabby

Aiming a little high there, aren't ya?

Sammy

Don't haze me!

Roxanna

(*To Duane.*) Do you have someone to take care of you tomorrow night or are you going to be all alone?

Duane

Are *you* going to be all alone?

Roxanna looks at Duane with "puppy dog" eyes.

Roxanna

(*To Duane.*) Yes, all by my lonesome. (*She sighs.*) Maybe I'll light a candle, write some poetry…or do some volunteer work at the orphanage. But I'm not thinking of myself. I'm worried about your fragile little heart, with no one to comfort you. IS THERE SOMEONE TO COMFORT YOU TOMORROW NIGHT?!?!?

Squirrel
Duane, please stick to the detention "rules" that we "discussed" earlier today.

Duane
(*To Squirrel.*) Would you lay off, man? I'm trying to concentrate! (*He turns back to Roxanna.*) When you use the words "tomorrow night," are you talking about the Prom?

Stanky and Scabby surround Sammy.

Stanky
(*To Scabby.*) I got a mouth full of spit and a fresh little Samantha princess right in front of me. What should I do, Scabby?

Scabby
Do what your "true self" tells you, Stanky.

Stanky
(*Grabbing Sammy by the hair.*) My true self tells me to spit! This is what you get when you turn your back on friends!

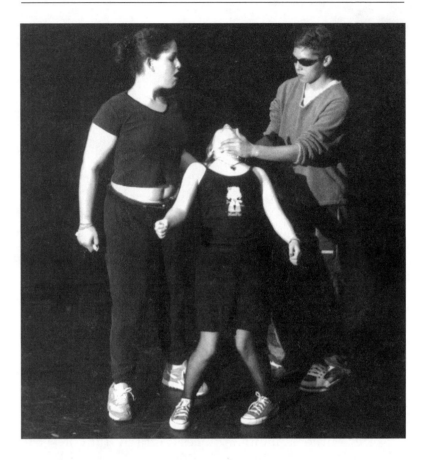

Sammy
Something tells me you're not my friends.

Duane
(*To Roxanna.*) I haven't asked anyone else to the Prom yet, if that's what you're trying to pull out of me.

Roxanna
Oh, Duane, you poor thing. You're going to suffer alone.

Duane

I know. Poor me.

Squirrel

(*Provoking.*) Duane, you're a stinky, smelly, ugly, dumb jock!

Stanky

(*To Sammy, about to spit.*) Open up and say AHHH!

Sammy

(*Blood-curdling and desperate, wrenching away from Stanky.*)
AAAAAAAAAAAAAAAHHHHHHHHHHH HHHHHHHHH!!!!!!!!!!!!

Everyone stares at Sammy. There is a pause.

Sammy

(*To Squirrel.*) May I go to the girls' room?

Squirrel

Why!?!

Sammy

Duh!

Squirrel

NO!

Sammy

Principal Touchstone always lets me! It's the law.

Squirrel
I NEED YOU HERE!

Sammy
SQUIRREL, I'M DESPERATE! PLEASE!

Squirrel
Fine, but hurry!

Sammy rushes out of the room.

Squirrel
Duane, I need you privately at my desk right this minute!

Duane
All right!

Squirrel goes back to his desk. Duane begins to follow Squirrel but Daisy stops him mid-way.

Daisy
Duane! Look at this picture of you slamming some guy on his head!

Duane
(*Easily distracted.*) Oh, wow, look at me.

Daisy
Wrestling city finals.

Duane
First place!

Roxanna
Duane!

Squirrel
(*From his desk.*) Duane!

Stanky and Scabby cross to Roxanna and pounce.

Stanky
(*To Roxanna.*) What the hell are you wearing?

Roxanna
What the hell are *you* wearing?

Scabby
So you want the hunk back, you poser? Well, FYI Princess, he got on his knees and begged me to go with him, but I said "no" 'cause I won't support sexist traditions! Why don't you do something real and boycott the Prom, like me. Make a statement for once!

Roxanna
MAKE A STATEMENT?!? You're telling me to make a statement? Look in the mirror! I feel sorry for posers like you floating around pretending to hate boys and the girls who get them. The scary part is you'll meet tons more phonies at American High. You'll swarm together like maggots and think that wearing black means you're making a statement, but that's a lie! You won't ever do or say anything worthwhile, all your friendships will be based on misery and you'll always feel as empty on the inside as you look on the outside. That's

why Duane—or any ordinary guy for that
matter—will never so much as give you a
smile...even though you desperately want one!

Duane
(*Still looking at his picture.*) Look how the sweat
glistens on my arm.

Daisy
You look totally awesome.

Duane
Totally.

Squirrel
DUANE! PRIVATELY, PLEASE!

Roxanna
Duane...

Squirrel
DUANE!

Roxanna
DUANE!

Sammy rushes back in dressed as a guy.

Sammy/Guy
DUANE!!!!!

Duane
Oh, hey, man...look at this sweet picture of me.

Sammy/Guy
Duane, my boy, how's our deal going? Did you ask her yet or what?

Squirrel
(*To Sammy/Guy.*) Excuse me, you can't just saunter into The Hole. You have to be forced here.

Sammy/Guy
I wouldn't come here and look at your joke of a face if it wasn't life or death.

Daisy
(*To Sammy/Guy.*) You look familiar but I don't have a Piranha picture of you. What's your name?

Sammy/Guy
Uh...Guy. Guy...Man...field...son.

Squirrel
Guy Manfieldson? Who are you—do you go to school here?

Sammy/Guy
No I...uh...go to Private Junior High across town. It's much better; you get to really focus on your studies. Kids know who they are and what they want. No confusing social pressures like Public.

Daisy
But I never forget a face. I know that I know you.

Daisy begins digging though her photos.

Sammy/Guy
Duane, listen to me. Did you ask her or not?

Duane
Who?

Sammy
Duane, I thought you were going to ask my sweet, honest Samantha to the Prom!

Duane
Oh, yeah.

Roxanna
You were, Duane?

Duane
As a matter of fact, YES! How do ya like that, Roxanna?!

Roxanna
Oh…I see…okay. If asking that scruffy girl makes you happy…then you should ask her.

Roxanna cries softly, like a sweet ingenue.

Duane
Oh, no, don't cry, Roxanna. Please don't cry.

Sammy/Guy
Duane, listen to the Queen. She's telling you to ask Samantha! (*To Roxanna.*) WHO IS NOT SCRUFFY!

Everyone FREEZES. Scabby steps forward.

Scabby
(*Aside.*) Roxanna's words are ringing in my
ears! She's right! I spew gallons but say
nothing! If I really want to make a statement,
if I really want to change old traditions, I have
to do something…real! And this strange
young dude's presence gives me a funny kind
of courage!

The FREEZE is broken by a wail from Roxanna.

Duane
(*Crying, to Roxanna.*) Don't cry. You know that
kills me. Please.

Roxanna
(*Crying.*) My feelings don't matter. Ask
Sammy to the Prom if it makes you happy.

Sammy/Guy
Yes! Ask Samantha.

Squirrel
DON'T ASK SAMANTHA! DUANE, DON'T
ASK SAMANTHA!

Sammy/Guy
Come on, man! You promised. I'll go get her!
Okay?

Sammy/Guy begins to exit, but Scabby stops her.

Scabby

Listen, you don't know me, and I don't know you...but will you go to the Prom with me?

Stanky and Sammy/Guy

What?!?

Scabby

I mean, I'll take you. I'll pay for dinner, the tickets—I'll even rent you a tux if you want.

Sammy/Guy

Oh, uh...

Roxanna wails.

Duane

Oh, poor Roxanna...you're so pure and sweet.

Squirrel

ASK ROXANNA AGAIN, DUANE! PLEASE!

Sammy/Guy

No! Don't fall for it, Duane! She's faking! Look at the way she's dressed, man. She's pretending to be someone she's not!

Scabby

(*To Sammy/Guy.*) If you think I'm insane, I understand, but I'll be the first girl at Public ever to take a guy to The Prom. That means a lot to me—and you seem cool...I kinda feel like I know you...

Stanky
Hey, Scabby, what about the Ms. Fits? What about me?

Scabby
Stanky, I'm destroying old conventions…I have to do this.

Duane
Roxanna, I'll do anything for you. You break my heart. Will you…will you…

Sammy/Guy
Don't ask her! ROXANNA! Will you go to the Prom with me?

Roxanna
What?

Scabby
What?!?

Duane
WHAT!?!?

Sammy/Guy
Will you go to the Prom with me?

Scabby
(*To Sammy/Guy.*) I guess I'm not pretty enough for you.

Duane
(*To Sammy/Guy.*) YOU LIED TO ME! YOU TOLD ME YOU WOULDN'T ASK ROXANNA!

Sammy/Guy
Well, you lied to me. You told me you'd ask
Samantha! What do you say, Roxanna?

Roxanna
(*To Duane.*) Are you going to ask that Sammy?
Because if you are, I'll accept this little guy's
invite. It's up to you.

Pause.

Sammy/Guy
(*Aside.*) Can somebody out there please tell me
what I'm doing?

Squirrel
Duane, please, I turned down Harvard so I
could go to high school with Samantha!

Sammy/Guy
What! You turned down Harvard?

Duane
I don't know who is being honest or who is
telling lies. I have to think.

*Duane assumes a wrestling stance and thinks. Silence.
More silence. Never-ending silence.*

Daisy
(*Holding up a photo.*) Here's that photo of
Sammy I love so much... My best friend!

Duane
(*To Roxanna.*) You would actually go with this
twerp?

Roxanna
At this point, why not?

Duane
FINE! I'm taking Samantha.

Roxanna
FINE! (*To Sammy/Guy.*) It's you and me, twerp.
Pick me up at six sharp! I want red roses.

Sammy/Guy
Uh...uh...okay...I guess.

Duane
Where is that chick anyway?

Sammy/Guy
I guess I'll go find her.

Squirrel
This is a blatant breach of contract, Duane! I
want my four hundred bucks back!

Duane
Fine! I'll hit you already, just leave me alone!

Squirrel
No, wait, not yet! She's not here!

Duane slugs Squirrel in the face. Everyone gasps in shock.

Sammy/Guy
(*Running to Squirrel.*) Squirrel? Are you okay?
Squirrel, wake up...Squirrel!

Daisy

(Screaming in terror.)
AAAAHHHHGGGGHHHH! (*To Sammy/Guy.*)
Oh, my God. I know who you are.

Daisy grabs a photo from her binder, then looks back at Sammy/Guy, then back at the photo and then back again at Sammy/Guy. It begins to dawn on the others.

Scabby

Oh, no...

Stanky

Oh, yes!

Roxanna

Oh, gross...

Duane

What? I don't get it. Who is he?

Roxanna crosses to Sammy/Guy and pulls off her fake goatee and hat.

Daisy

AAAAAAAAAAHHHHHHHHHHHGGGGG
GGGHHHHHH!!!!!!!!!!

Duane

OH, SICK MAN!!! SICK!!!!

Tabatha Sue and Amanda Lou enter skipping and throwing confetti over everyone!

Tabatha Sau and Amanda Lou
26!26! 26 HOURS! 26 HOURS 'TIL PROM!
ROCK ON! ROCK ON CHAKA KHAN! 26
HOURS 'TIL PROM!

They exit skipping! Silence.

Sammy
Somebody help Squirrel. He's passed out
cold!

Scabby
Sammy. What. Are. You. Doing?

Duane
Why are you dressed up like a guy? What is
this?

Sammy
Why'd you clock him in the face, Duane?

Duane
He paid me four hundred bucks to clock him
in the face. He did it for you.

Sammy
For me?

Duane
Yeah. He wanted to work the pity angle so
you'd go to the Prom with him.

Sammy
Oh, Squirrel.

Roxanna
(*To Sammy.*) Why are you stealing my
boyfriend, you greaseball?

Scabby
Seriously! Who do you think you are, Sammy?

Sammy
I...I...I...

Sammy looks to the audience.

Sammy (*cont'd*)
(*Aside.*) I should have said yes to poor
Squirrel. I'd have a rose corsage...I'd have a
real friend...he'd be conscious now...

Roxanna
(*To Sammy.*) WHO DO YOU THINK YOU
ARE!?!

Sammy
(*Snapping.*) I DON'T KNOW! I DON'T
KNOW! I DON'T KNOW WHO I AM!!! I
wanted...I just wanted to be a Queen.

Daisy
Awwww. I just love ya'll so much. I'll never
forget ya'll.

Roxanna
There's only one Prom Queen and that's me!
Don't you forget it! And believe me when I
tell you: everyone, I mean everyone next year
will know about your schizophrenic identity

crisis! You just dug yourself into the deepest freak hole in the history of American High!

Sammy
(*Sarcastic.*) Thanks for understanding.

Scabby
You can't toy with people's feelings, Sammy!

Sammy
Look who's talking!

Duane
(*To Sammy.*) You're the one who treated me like a human trophy. I'M SO MUCH MORE THAN JUST A HUNK!

Sammy
Does anyone care that Squirrel is practically dead?

Everyone
Nope.

Roxanna
But Duane…? I wonder…is it right to break someone's face for four hundred dollars? I mean, is it moral?

Stanky
Moral? Moral? Did the word moral slip through your hypocritical plastic lips?!?!

Roxanna
My goodness, it did! For some reason I feel so

grounded in...morality. (*Surprised.*) IT'S
THESE FLATS!!!

Duane

Roxanna, I broke his face for you, so I could
get you a beautiful black limousine. But he—
(*Referring to Sammy.*)—she—*it*—told me you
didn't like me for me, whatever that means.

Roxanna

It was right. This morning—when we were
going to the Prom together—I was a really
selfish young lady who only cared about her
beauty. But I now know that it's about going
with someone whose heart you totally, totally,
totally, totally like.

Duane

Really? That's what I think, too!

Roxanna

Really? Oh...

*Long pause. Finally Roxanna clears her throat — a signal for
Duane to ask her to the Prom.*

Duane

(*Finally getting the hint.*) Roxanna, do you
think you could postpone your volunteer
work at the orphanage and go to the Prom
with me?

Roxanna

Oh, Duane! Oh, yes!

Duane

All right!

Daisy

(*Aside.*) Who knew that all the warm friendship I've been searching for was here in detention the whole time.

Roxanna and Duane begin to exit together.

Duane

I'm going to get you the biggest limo they have!

Roxanna

OKAY!

Sammy

Duane…I'm sorry.

Duane

Me, too, Scruffy. You should have just asked me…I might have said yes.

Roxanna slaps him on the arm.

Sammy

(*To Duane, referring to Squirrel.*) Maybe you should give him his four hundred bucks back. I mean, you did break his face.

Duane walks over to Squirrel, who is still out cold.

Duane

(*Pulling out the wad of cash and dropping it on Squirrel.*) Here's eleven bucks.

Duane turns to exit.

Duane (*cont'd*)
(*To Roxanna.*) The cool thing about a limo is
it's got space for two hundred wine coolers.

Duane and Roxanna exit.

Daisy
(*Referring to Squirrel's face.*) Ya'll, his nose is the
size of a softball.

Stanky
Cool! It looks like a giant goose egg.

Sammy
Squirrel, can you hear me? Squirrel?

Squirrel wakes.

Squirrel
(*Overly dramatic.*) Is that you, Samantha?

Sammy
Squirrel, are you okay?

Squirrel
(*Puckering up his lips for a kiss.*) Samantha,
come closer.

Sammy
What are you doing?

Squirrel
The only thing in the world that could right

this disastrous wrong is if you would go to the
Prom with me.

Sammy
You need to go to Nurse Ratchet, Squirrel.
Your face looks like Humpty Dumpty.

Daisy
(*Helping Squirrel to his feet.*) I'll take him.

Squirrel
(*To Sammy.*) So what time should I pick you
up tomorrow night?

Sammy
I can't go, Squirrel. I can't show my face.

Squirrel
If I can, you can.

Sammy
You shouldn't have turned down Harvard.
Not for me, at least.

Squirrel
What about our friendship?

Sammy
Our friendship fizzled when you got on your
power trip. Stop playing Sheriff.

Squirrel
When you stop playing punk. (*To the others.*)
Anyone else here want to go to the Prom with

me? (*Pause.*) Going once? (*Pause.*) Going twice? (*Pause.*) Sold? (*Pause.*) Well, my loss.

Daisy
Squirrel, you gotta let me take a picture of your nose. The memories will last forever.

Squirrel
Great.

Daisy
Oh, Sammy, I'm still going to print your quotation...'cause I think you really meant it.

Daisy pulls another flower out of her hair and tosses it to Sammy. Squirrel and Daisy exit.

Stanky
Well, you stinky losers, it looks like it's the three of us and a bottle of vodka. Unless you two still want to go to the Prom together.

Scabby
SHUT UP!

Stanky
Now that would be a statement! I don't know what it says, but it says something.

Sammy
Scabby, go ask a guy, any guy, it doesn't matter. Take him to the Prom and have a great time. Just quit lying about everything.

Stanky

You're the liar, Samantha.

Sammy

I almost got asked to the Prom by Duane the Hunk! The Captain of the wrestling team! Is it too much to wanna be someone?!?

Stanky

If you think going out with Dumb Jock Duane makes you someone, then you're even more of a fake than I thought. You're a bigger fake than all of the fakes put together in this asylum.

Sammy

Well, I don't know what else to do! School is a lonely waste of pointless life. I hate it.

Stanky

Yeah, it reeks — and high school is gonna be worse, so get used to it!

Sammy

Well, I don't want it to reek! I want it to be special. I want to get up in the morning for something besides black eye liner and chains. I want to do something...love something... *someone*. Is that too much to ask?

Stanky

Yes.

A bell rings. Lights up on Tabatha Sue and Amanda Lou behind their microphones. Stanky, Scabby and Sammy listen.

Tabatha Sue

Well, Piranhas, Public Junior High will be closing in five minutes, so scadattle the heck out of here and get your beautiful selves to…you know where!

Amanda Lou

We just want to take this special moment to shout out a personal "hey" to our Prom dates. You know who you are.

Tabatha Sue

To my special guy…I want to say thank you for being so sweet, and for asking me to the dance.

Amanda Lou

And to my sweetie pie…you mean so much to me, and this weekend would be totally heinous if I couldn't spend it with you.

Tabatha Sue

Sure, my dress, the dinner, the dancing, the pictures, the flowers are all exciting…

Amanda Lou

…but the specialty is you. See you tomorrow night.

Tabatha Sue and Amanda Lou
AND THAT'S THE SCOOP!

Tabatha Sue

This is a gloriously giddy Tabatha Sue…

Amanda Lou
...and a super silly Amanda Lou for...

Tabatha Sue and Amanda Lou
...Public Junior High.

Amanda Lou
PEACE!

Tabatha Sue
OUT!

Lights out on Tabatha Sue and Amanda Lou.

Scabby
(*Listening, inspired.*) I'm gonna take Squirrel!

Stanky
What?!?! You traitor!

Sammy
Oh, wow! Go for it!

Stanky
You wimp! You wimp! You'll be sorry when I haze your face tomorrow night!

Scabby
At least I won't be alone!

Sammy
Hurry, Scabby!

Scabby
Wish me luck!

Stanky
I CURSE THE DAY WE EVER MET!

Scabby exits, running.

Stanky *(cont'd)*
(*Enraged.*) Where's she gonna get the money for a dress? I'm goin' home.

Sammy
You gonna get drunk?

Stanky
All by myself. And I'm gonna have a blast! SO HAH! HAH! HAH! HAAAAAAH! HAAAA AAAAAAAAAAAAAAAAAAAAAA...!

Stanky thrashes around the room violently!

Stanky (*cont'd*)
...HAAAAAAAAAAAAAAAAAAAAAAAAA
AAAAAAAAAAH!

Sammy
You need therapy!

Stanky
SO DO YOU!

Stanky exits. Francois enters, out of breath from running.

Francois
Oh, great fortune! I caught you!

Sammy
I blew it, Francois. And anyway, I was an idiot
to think it would work in the first place.

Francois
May I beg a moment of your time to tell you
about a very exciting opportunity?

Sammy
What?

Francois
Next year I'm starting my own acting troupe
named The American High Freshmen Players.
I would be honored if you would grace my
company with your membership.

Sammy
Why?

Francois
I think you're awesome, Samantha. Your instincts are red hot, your emotionality is available and your willingness to commit your whole self is priceless.... Please, consider committing your whole self to me — uh — I mean — to my group.

Sammy
What, we do, like, plays?

Francois
We'll play up any play your playful heart must play out.

Pause. Sammy considers.

Sammy
Hey, Francois?

Francois
Yes?

Sammy
What happens to that girl at the end of *As You Like It?*

Francois
Oh, um... Well, Rosalind sheds her disguise and reveals her true self...as a woman. She gets her guy and lives happily ever after.

Pause. Sammy considers.

Sammy
Well... If we keep the acting in the theatre...your play group sounds...playable.

Francois
A thousand thank you's...Samantha.

Sammy
No, a thousand thank *you's*...Francois.

Francois
A thousand thank you's.

Sammy
A thousand a thousand thank you's. So...
do you want to give me a flyer for your show
tomorrow night or what?

Francois
Really? Oh, yes, by all means!

He hands her a flyer.

Francois (*cont'd*)
It might just be you and me there...but still
lots of fun. There'll be sodas, and my mom's
making those mini pizza bagels.

Sammy
Oh, yeah, those are cool.

Francois
So maybe we'll meet tomorrow evening...

Sammy
Maybe we will...

A moment. They smile at one another.

Francois
Ciao, good lady.

Sammy
Ciao. (*Pause.*) Oh, Francois…?

Francois
Yes, Samantha?

Sammy
…Break a leg!

Francois exits. Sammy sits alone. She grabs the fake goatee off the floor and puts it in her pocket.

Lights fade.

THE END

About the author…

Josh Adell has been teaching acting to children since 1990, in Dallas, New York and Los Angeles. Upon graduating from New York University he taught with Global Volunteers in Tver, Russia, where he wrote and directed the children's show *Wild Thing*. As an actor Josh has worked with the Dallas Children's Theatre, Playwrights Horizons in New York and is a member of the Interact Theatre Company in North Hollywood, California. Josh currently has a blast teaching Voice and Comedy Improvisation at Class Act's Young Actor's Studio.

SUMMER

by Gideon Brower

SUMMER was written as a commissioned work for Class Act's Young Actor's Studio. It was directed by Jeff Alan-Lee and Kerry Muir and produced July 1997 at The Ventura Court Theatre in Studio City with the following cast:

CAST

Older Alice......................................Tess Siedman

Alice...Alison Shafer

Paul..Andrew Shafer

Joey...Gary Ohanian

Shawna...Clara Hauser

Sam..Morgan Lewis

Claire...Agnes Hewitt

Gina..Galina Zukhov

Jeffrey...Jaime Vazquez

The play can be performed on a bare stage with a minimum of props.

Bare stage. The Narrator, also called "Older Alice," 13, enters.

Narrator/Older Alice
I grew up in a little town. I guess I'm still growing up in it. It's one of those places most people only see driving through on their way to somewhere else. They look out the window and see a place where nothing interesting ever happens. I used to see that, too, and I live here. But the summer I was nine, some things happened to change my mind. I'm not going to tell you about it, though. Instead, I'll show you how it happened.

The Narrator walks over to where a nine-year-old version of herself stands listening impatiently.

Narrator
This is me when I was nine. I guess I was a pretty average kid.

Alice
Is this gonna take a long time?

Narrator
Maybe a little impatient sometimes.

Narrator walks over to where Paul, 11, stands wearing an ice cream uniform shirt with "Jason" stitched on the pocket.

Narrator (*cont'd*)
This is my older brother Paul. He was eleven.

Paul sneezes, blows his nose.

Narrator (*cont'd*)
Paul's outstanding feature was his allergies.
He was allergic to dust. Pollen. Ragweed.
Cats.

Paul edges away from an unseen cat, waving his arms.

Paul
Go away! Shoo!

Narrator
Paul usually spent his time at home, reading.
But that summer he got a job scooping ice
cream at the Baskin-Robbins. They gave him a
lot of responsibility. But it wasn't always easy.

The Narrator watches as Joey, 8, walks up to Paul.

Joey
I'll take Rocky Road, Paul. With nuts.

Paul
(*Scooping.*) Do I know you?

Joey
I've seen you around. How much?

Paul
A dollar-fifty.

Joey
How 'bout you give me a discount, Paul?

Paul
I'm not giving you a discount. And quit
calling me Paul.

Joey
You can't put it back now, Paul. It's all mixed
together. I'll give you a dollar for it.

Paul
It's a dollar-fifty!

Joey
That's a shame. Looks like you're gonna have
to waste it, then.

Paul realizes Joey's got his number.

Paul
All right, give me the dollar.

Joey
Thanks, Paul. See you later.

Paul
Get lost. And quit calling me Paul!

*Alice, Shawna and Samantha - called Sam - (all age 9) sprawl
nearby, playing cards. Sam is completely limp in the heat.
Narrator walks over and sits next to them.*

Narrator
Me and my friends Shawna and Samantha

mostly just lay around and played cards. It seemed like it was too hot to do anything else.

Alice
Got any sixes?

Shawna gives her one.

Alice
Thank you. Any nines?

Shawna
Go fish.

Alice
Sam, aren't you gonna play?

Sam
It's too hot.

Shawna
Too hot to play cards?

Sam
It's too hot to do anything.

Narrator
Our only real goal was to win the talent contest that was held every year before the Fourth of July dance. The problem was, we couldn't come up with an act.

Alice
I know. We could do a dance routine.

Shawna
What would we do?

Alice
I don't know. We could tap dance. Look. We just take a can and we crush it, see?

She crushes a can and dances around using it as a tap.

Alice *(cont'd)*
Huh? This is pretty good, don't you think? Come on! What do you think?

Shawna
(*Unenthused.*) Nah.

Sam
It's too hot to tap dance.

Narrator
The one person who actually could dance was my older sister, Claire. Claire had just turned fourteen. She was teaching herself from a tape. She really wasn't too bad.

Claire, 14, wearing a Walkman, moves around, counting.

Claire
One, two, three… one, two, three…

Narrator
Claire recorded all her daily activities in her diary –

A hand from offstage gives the Narrator a diary.

Narrator (*cont'd*)
— which I happen to have right here. (*Reads.*)
"Dear Diary. Today I got up and went outside.
Ate lunch. Worked on dancing. It's very hot.
When will anything ever happen to me?"
(*Looks up.*) Claire was not having the most
interesting summer.

Narrator looks over at the sprawled-out girls and Paul, who is reading behind the counter of the Baskin-Robbins.

Narrator (*cont'd*)
None of us were. But that changed when Gina
came into the ice cream store. Gina was a year
older than us. We knew her a little bit, but she
went to a different school.

Gina, 10, enters Paul's ice cream store.

Gina
Hi.

Paul
Hi. Excuse me one minute.

Paul steps into the back room, where the Narrator holds up a mirror. Paul takes a comb from his pocket and runs it through his hair.

Narrator
One thing I forgot to tell you about Paul, along
with his allergies: he fell in love a lot. One
minute he'd be fine. The next, kaboom. It was
embarrassing.

In the store, Gina looks around at Alice, Shawna and Sam.

Gina

Hi.

Alice, Shawna, Sam

Hey.

Paul steps back behind the counter.

Paul

Can I help you?

Gina

Chocolate. One scoop.

Paul

Gotcha.

Paul starts scooping.

Paul (cont'd)

Chocolate. That's a very popular flavor.
Vanilla, that's the other big one. You like
vanilla?

Gina

I like chocolate better.

Paul

Yeah. Me too. You want anything on that?
Sprinkles? Crushed almonds?

Gina

No.

Paul hands over the ice cream.

Paul

Good. Right. Just chocolate. That says it all.
Vanilla is actually more popular, on a national
basis. I read an article on it recently. I
personally sell more vanilla.

Gina

How much is it?

Paul

Um – a dollar. (*She pays.*) Thanks. Come back
anytime. In the afternoon, three to six. Ask for
Paul.

Gina

Your shirt says Jason.

Paul

What? Oh. Right. It used to be somebody else's shirt. Bye.

The girls look on as Paul goes to the door and watches Gina walk away.

Alice

Oh, God. I suppose he's in love now.

Shawna

He's always in love with somebody.

Paul

I am not.

Sam

Yes you are. You're famous for it.

Paul

I am not!

Narrator

He was, though. Everybody knew Paul fell in love on a daily, even hourly basis. He had a heart like a pincushion.

Paul

(*To Narrator.*) Don't say that. It's not true.

Narrator

No? Remember second grade? You kept saying you were sick because you had a crush on the nurse?

Paul
Okay, one time.

Narrator
Fourth grade? You sent Miss Biddle those Valentine cards?

Paul
Everyone sent her Valentines.

Narrator
Not in October.

Paul
Yeah, well. This is different.

Narrator
If you say so.

Older Alice walks over to where Claire is practicing her dancing.

Claire
One, two, three…

Narrator
As I said, Claire was having another summer of incredible dullness. But things were about to change for her also.

Claire stops. The Narrator is in her way.

Narrator (*cont'd*)
(*Steps aside.*) Sorry. Go ahead.

Claire continues dancing.

Claire
One, two, three... one, two, three... one, two... one, two...

Jeffrey
(*Offstage, from up in a tree.*) You forgot three.

Claire
Who is that?

Jeffrey, 15, climbs down from the tree.

Jeffrey
I didn't mean to scare you. If I did. I'm not
saying I did. But if I did, I didn't mean to. I'm
Jeffrey, by the way. I'm new in town. That's a
cliché, but it's true. I'm visiting for the
summer.

Claire
I'm Claire. What were you doing up in the tree?

Jeffrey
Oh, just watching life go by. I find it's helpful
to remove yourself from the hustle-bustle once
in a while. It's very inspiring to be in that tree.
Isn't it amazing, when you think about it, that
the maple tree is so beautiful, and not only
that, but the sap from it can feed people? The
maple tree. It's a wonderful thing, a miracle of
nature.

Claire
I think that's an elm.

Jeffrey
(*Surprised.*) Really? Well, elms are good too,
you know. I think of them as an honest
American tree. Maples are more of a Canadian

kind of thing. Although still a fine tree, of
course. I could stay up there all day. Just
listening to the sounds of the town. You ever
do that? Just listen?

Claire

Sometimes I get up early. I like to walk
around. It's so quiet.

Jeffrey

Exactly! That's just what I mean. You seem
like a very observant person, Claire. Tell me
something, do you think I talk a lot?

Claire

Yes.

Jeffrey

I appreciate your honesty. That's important in
a person. Where are you headed?

Claire

The library.

Jeffrey

I've never been there. Maybe I'll walk over
there with you. *(They walk.)* I think you've got
real talent as a dancer. I'm no expert, though.
I'm more of a verbal type person.

Claire

I can tell.

*They walk away. The Narrator crosses as Alice comes in with
a pamphlet and beanbags.*

Narrator
All this time, the three of us were still trying to work out what to do for the talent show.

Alice
All right, I have another idea. We'll juggle. Look, I got a book that shows you how to do it. (*Demonstrates.*) You just throw one beanbag up. Okay. Now throw two up. Now three. See? (*The bags fall down.*) Okay, maybe I'm not very good yet, but I'm getting there. What do you think?

Shawna
Nah.

Sam
(*Flat on her back.*) It's too hot to juggle.

Narrator walks over to where Gina is playing an unidentifiable tune on the recorder. Paul stands nearby.

Narrator
As for Gina, she was a very nice girl. Was she a musician? No. But Paul didn't notice. He was determined to make this romance work out. He made up a checklist of things to do.

Paul stands, reading over his checklist. He doesn't notice Joey standing nearby.

Paul
(*Reads.*) One. Find out her interests. Two.

Discuss them with her. Three. Make a romantic gesture.

Joey
What's a romantic gesture?

Paul
Go away.

Joey
This is about that girl Gina, isn't it? I heard you liked her.

Paul
What are you, the CIA? Get lost.

Joey shrugs and wanders off. Gina finishes her song. Paul claps when she's done, walks over.

Paul (cont'd)
Hi. Remember me? From the ice cream store. Paul. (*Points to his chest.*) Remember, it says Jason, but it's Paul.

Gina
I'm Gina.

Paul
I know. (*Re: her playing.*) Is that for the talent show?

Gina
Yes. Could you tell what it was?

Paul

(*Enthusiastic.*) What, are you kidding? Of course! (*Gina waits.*) Um... "Twinkle Twinkle, Little Star?"

Gina

(*Disappointed.*) It's supposed to be "Hot Cross Buns."

Paul

Right! That's what I meant to say. It sounded great.

Gina

I should go home.

Paul

Why don't I walk you? Okay?

Gina

If you want.

They start walking.

Paul

So you're interested in music. Are you going to the dance after the talent show?

Gina

I guess. (*Stops.*) Well. Here we are.

Paul

Here? You live right here?

Gina
Yes.

Paul
It was nice talking to you. (*Hesitates, then:*)
About the dance. Would you like to go with me?

Gina
I don't think so. See you.

She exits. Paul stands there, disappointed. He sneezes. Joey walks up.

Joey
Nice going, buddy.

Joey exits. The three girls listen as the Narrator continues.

Narrator
The next part of our story needs a little explanation. Ready? A year before all this happened, our parents took us to see an Italian movie about a boy who falls in love. The girl won't talk to him. So he stands in the street outside her house. It rains, it snows. Finally she realizes she loves him. She runs into his arms. It's very romantic.

Shawna
(*To Narrator.*) Wait a second. How long does he stand out there?

Narrator
Weeks. Maybe months.

Sam
How's he go to the bathroom?

Narrator
I don't know. It wasn't in the movie. May I continue?

Shawna
Sorry.

Narrator
When Gina wouldn't go to the dance with him, Paul remembered the movie. And he decided to take some bold action.

Paul walks up. He indicates the chair the Narrator is seated on.

Paul
Can I borrow this chair?

Narrator
What for?

Paul
To win the heart of the woman I love.

Narrator stands. Paul takes the chair, walks away, turns.

Paul (*cont'd*)
I'll bring it back when I'm done.

He exits.

Narrator
But none of this solved our problem of what to do for the talent show.

> ### *Shawna*
>
> I know what we can do. We'll do a modern dance.

> ### *Alice*
>
> What's that?

> ### *Shawna*
>
> You know. You dance around and you play finger cymbals and it's about something.

> ### *Sam*
>
> Like what?

> ### *Shawna*
>
> Anything. Name a subject.

> ### *Sam*
>
> How about, "It's really, really hot."

> ### *Shawna*
>
> Okay.

She performs a dance using the cymbals.

> ### *Shawna (cont'd)*
>
> See? Try another subject.

> ### *Alice*
>
> How about, "This is a dumb idea."

> ### *Shawna*
>
> Okay.

Again she dances around, clacking the cymbals.

Shawna (*cont'd*)

You try it.

Alice

No, thanks.

Sam

It's too hot to do modern dance.

Narrator

Meanwhile, at the library, Jeffrey and Claire were in trouble. Big trouble.

Narrator puts on reading glasses and sternly points the way out to Jeffrey and Claire.

Narrator (*cont'd*)

Talking can not be tolerated in the library.

Jeffrey and Claire walk away from the library.

Claire

I've never been kicked out of the library before. It was kind of exciting.

Jeffrey

You're not mad? That's good. I don't know what comes over me. It's verbosity. Blah, blah, blah, all the time. My mother sent me to a shrink because of it. He said I was going through a phase. You know, like the moon.

Claire

My parents say I don't talk enough.

Jeffrey
They do? That's wrong. You say a lot without talking. Not everyone does, but you do. Plus it means more when you do say something.

They come upon Paul sitting in his chair, surrounded by Alice, Shawna and Sam. Joey sits nearby.

Jeffrey (cont'd)
What's going on here? (*Notices Narrator.*) Excuse me? Miss? Could you tell me what's happening?

Narrator
Haven't you been paying attention?

Claire
(*Apologetic.*) We were at the library.

Narrator
(*Sighs.*) Oh, all right. Paul asked Gina to go to the dance. She said no. So he's waiting for her to come out. He's going to wait as long as it takes.

Claire
Don't tell me he's in love again.

Narrator shrugs, turns to Joey. He considers.

Joey
I see it as more of a childish infatuation.

Alice and her friends are gathered around Paul.

Alice

You're really going to sit here until Gina goes to the dance with you?

Paul

Yes.

Shawna

What if she doesn't want to?

We hear the sound of Gina practicing "Hot Cross Buns" on her recorder.

Paul

Hush! The beautiful music of the woman I adore.

Sam

Oh my God. I thought it was a cat.

Alice

What if she doesn't come out? You're just gonna sit here?

Shawna

They'll have to mow the lawn around you. The grass you're sitting on will get higher and higher until you completely disappear. When they finally come looking for you, they'll just find a skeleton.

Paul thinks about this.

Paul

I'll take that chance.

Sam

Good luck, soldier.

The girls walk away, passing Narrator.

Narrator

All this time, the urgent question of the talent show was still unresolved. And time was rapidly running out.

Alice

(*Irritated, to Narrator.*) All right already! We're working on it!

Narrator

Sorry. Go ahead.

Sam

I think we should sing.

Shawna

What are you talking about? Who's gonna sing? None of us can sing.

Sam

I can sing.

Alice

No you can't. Sing something.

Sam sings briefly. The others are impressed.

Alice

That's not bad. You know some other songs?

> ### Sam
> Sure.

> ### Shawna
> Okay, but what are *we* gonna do?

> ### Alice
> I'll think of something. Hmm. I need an idea.
> Hmm. (*Pointedly, to Narrator.*) *I need an idea.*

Narrator catches on, goes over and whispers in her ear. Alice nods.

> ### Alice (*cont'd*)
> I've got it!

She confers with the others.

> ### Narrator
> And so it was that we came up with the act we
> finally performed. Ladies and gentlemen,
> please welcome…Samantha, Shawna and
> Alice.

She steps back as the three girls perform a number: Sam sings, Shawna and Alice sing backup, tap dance and play finger cymbals. Narrator hands them a trophy. They bow and run off.

The Narrator steps forward.

> ### Narrator (*cont'd*)
> And after the talent show, the dance. I
> suppose you're wondering what happened to
> Paul and Gina. Did she go to the dance with

him? I'm afraid the news is not good.
(*Encouraging, to Gina.*) Come on out. It's okay.

Gina steps out of her house. She walks up to Paul.

Paul

Hi.

Gina

Hi. Listen...it's nice of you to wait out here
like this. I mean, it's weird, but it's nice. I
think. But I'm going to the dance with Robert.
I told him I would, last week. Sorry.

She puts something into Paul's hand.

Gina (*cont'd*)

I brought you something. Bye.

She walks away. Paul stares down at the object in his hand.

Narrator

What is it?

Paul

(*Mortified.*) A cookie.

Narrator

Really? Well...it's better than nothing. Right?

Paul

(*Walks after Gina.*) Wait! There's something I
have to know.

Narrator

Don't do it, Paul. You'll be sorry.

Paul

If I had asked you first, would you have gone with me?

Gina

Um...well...no. Sorry.

She exits.

Narrator

I told him not to ask.

Paul

(*Calls after Gina.*) You'll change your mind! You'll be back! And I'll be here!

He collapses back onto his chair.

Narrator

And did she change her mind? First, let's see what's happening with Claire and Jeffrey. Jeffrey left the dance before it started. And where did Claire find him when she went to look for him? You guessed it.

Claire stands looking up at Jeffrey, who is back in his tree.

Claire

What are you doing there?

Jeffrey

Nothing.

Claire
Why don't you come down?

Jeffrey
I'm fine up here.

Claire
Can I come up?

Jeffrey
If you want.

She climbs up and joins him in the tree.

Claire
Why did you leave?

Jeffrey
(*Shrugs, uncomfortable.*) I don't know. It was
just...when I got there and there were all those
people there... and I didn't know anybody
and I didn't see you. I just didn't feel like
staying. You know that feeling, when you just
can't seem to talk to anybody?

Claire
Yes.

Jeffrey
The truth is, I'm not really that good with
people. With you, I'm okay. But with most
people...I told you, it's a phase I'm going
through.

Claire
Me too. (*Pauses.*) Can I ask you a personal question?

Jeffrey
Sure.

Claire
Have you ever been in love?

Jeffrey
Yes. I was in love with Ingrid Bergman for a while.

Claire
Does she live around here?

Jeffrey
No. She was in movies. I never met her.

Claire
(*Considers.*) I think it means more if you know the person.

Jeffrey
Do you want to go back to the dance?

Claire
No.

Jeffrey
Neither do I.

Claire
We could have our own dance.

Jeffrey
What, a pretend dance?

Claire
A real dance. Come down. I'll show you.
Come on.

She climbs down. He follows.

Jeffrey
I don't know. I'm more of a verbal-type
person.

Claire
I'll show you. It's easy. Just move your foot
forward. That's it. Now count. One two
three, one two three, one two three...

Jeffrey counts also.

Claire (*cont'd*)
See, you're getting it.

They dance. Narrator moves to center stage.

Narrator
So, things seem to be wrapping up nicely. Did
Gina ever come back for Paul? Well...I'm
afraid not.

She walks over to where Paul sits glumly on his chair.

Narrator (*cont'd*)
How's it going there, Paul?

Paul

(*To Narrator.*) It's not fair. The girls win the contest. Claire and Jeffrey are happy. Gina's happy. How come I have to end up miserable and alone?

Narrator

Look on the bright side. You haven't sneezed once. Besides, you may be miserable, but you're definitely not alone.

Joey enters.

Joey

Come on, Paul. I'll buy you a soda.

Paul

(*Sighs.*) Oh, all right.

He stands. Joey picks up the chair. They walk away.

Joey

You know, Paul…this could be the beginning of a beautiful friendship.

They exit, leaving the Narrator alone on stage. Alice enters.

Alice

Well? Is it over?

Narrator

I still have to talk about the important lessons we learned the summer I was nine.

Alice

All right, make it fast.

Narrator

(*To audience.*) I learned that vanilla ice cream outsells chocolate on a national basis. And that romantic Italian movies aren't always realistic.

Alice

Big deal.

Narrator

I also learned that interesting things happen almost everywhere. Even in a town everybody

thinks is boring. Sometimes the things you have
to work hard to see are the most interesting of all.

Alice
(*Checks watch.*)   Okay, time's up.

Narrator
(*To audience.*) At least, I think so. I'm still
working on that last part.

*Alice holds out her hand insistently. Narrator takes it. They
exit together.*

Blackout.

THE END

About the author...

Gideon Brower is a comedian and screenwriter and a native
of Baltimore, Maryland. He is a member of the Los Angeles
Writers and Actors Lab.

BEFRIENDING BERTHA

by Kerry Muir

for Dimitri, the original "Charlie"
&
for Johnny

BEFRIENDING BERTHA was produced July 1995 at The Great Platte River Playwrights Festival in Kearney, Nebraska. It was directed by David Brandt with the following cast and crew:

CAST

Bertha	Jenae Frye
Tiny	Aubrey Brandt
Charlie	T.J. Ritchie
Pink	Fay Gallagher
Woman	Sara Schulte

CREW

Set	Ryan James Brehmer
Lighting	Rachel Nabel
Props	Jamie Haverkamp
Stage Manager	Sadie Brandt
Music (*Composer*)	Bettina Covo

BEFRIENDING BERTHA was produced August 1995 at the Nantucket Short Play Festival and Competition. It was directed by Marjory Trott with the following cast and crew:

CAST

Bertha.. Leah Day
Tiny... Meredith Shepherd
Charlie... Louis Howe
Pink... Misha Currie
Woman...Marjory Trott

CREW

Technical Support............................. Karina Rios
Emily Brown

Cast of Characters:

Bertha: .... So shy, she can barely speak. Wears glasses. Around age 11.

Tiny: .... Short, but fiesty. A realist. Around age 10.

Charlie: .... Maniacally talkative. Around age 12.

Pink: .... A wild-child. Somewhat of an outlaw. Around age 12.

Woman: .... Someone's mother, looking for her child.

Breakdown of Scenes:

Prologue
Scene one...................... "Luminosity"
Scene two...................... "Voyages"
Scene three................... "Pink"
Scene four..................... "Gypsy Spell"
Scene five..................... "Breakdown"
Scene six....................... "Transformation"
Scene seven................. "Resplendence"
Scene eight................... "Thoughts of Rio"
Scene nine.................... "Trouble at the Border"
Scene ten...................... "Stars"

Place:

*Each scene takes place at school, on the fringes of a play-
ground.*

Costumes:

*Bertha should wear something simple and drab; a white but-
ton up shirt with a Peter Pan collar and a gray or navy skirt,
white ankle high or knee-high socks and flat uninteresting
shoes. And maybe a cardigan sweater.*

*Charlie might sport a bow tie and some other accessory which
is slightly exotic. It might be a pair of high-top sneakers in
bright red. It might be a blazer.*

*Pink is flashy. She wears many beads, bracelets and some
sort of amazing hair clip (with a bow, an exotic flower, or
even some plastic fruit attached). She might carry a fan or a
scarf, have mismatched socks and temporary tattoos. When
creating Pink's costume, it should be remembered that her
influences are as follows: Madonna, Carmen Miranda, the
circus, Gloria Swanson, all silent film starlets, Mardi Gras,
James Dean, Carnivale in Brazil, Isadora Duncan, Vivian
Leigh (as both Scarlet O'Hara and Blanche DuBois), Elvis,
Rock 'n Roll, Grunge and film noir. She should be sparkly,
dreamy, elegant, flamboyant — - and at the same time, she
should look like she crawled out of a garbage can.*

Tiny shops at The Gap.

*The Woman is a beautician by profession, so she should be
nicely coifed, with a hip and earthy appearance. Nothing too
fancy; she's a working single mom.*

P R O L O G U E

Bertha is eating lunch alone on the playground. She is a quiet, shy girl, who is very shut down. She is actually pretty but completely lacks any self-confidence or belief in herself.

Tiny enters. She bounces a basketball. She stares at Bertha as she does this. Bertha does not move, just sits frozen.

Tiny stops bouncing the ball and sits down, still staring at Bertha. She starts doing strange sign language with her hands. Bertha does not know what to say.

Tiny stops the sign language, looks at Bertha, and snaps her fingers loudly right by Bertha's ear.

Bertha looks at her. After a moment:

Tiny
My sister says you're deaf.

Tiny picks up the basketball and leaves, bouncing the basketball as she goes. Bertha remains frozen. Lights fade out.

S C E N E   O N E :
"LUMINOSITY"

Lights up. Charlie enters suddenly from out of nowhere and sits by the frozen Bertha. He has a wild energy, sort of like a volcano that's about to explode. Bertha is shocked, remains frozen.

Charlie
(*As if nothing was out of the ordinary and they had been talking a while.*) See, that's the whole trouble with tuna fish. You eat it, your breath smells for maybe one, two, sometimes even three hours afterwards. There's a number of ways to deal with the problem. You can use Certs, Tic-Tacs…even Scope if you can find a little bottle in a convenient travel size. Potato chip? (*He offers her his bag.*)

Bertha
No thank you.

Charlie
Pickle?

Bertha shakes her head.

Charlie (*cont'd*)
Sip of cola? (*Pause.*) I seemed to have
frightened you.

Bertha shakes her head "no".

Charlie (*cont'd*)
No?

Bertha shakes head "no" again.

Charlie (*cont'd*)
Oh. Okay. Silent type. Good, we'll be great
friends. You can listen, and I'll do all the
talking. As I was saying… (*He looks at Bertha
who is still frozen.*) You know, for a girl of I
would say, 11 or 12 years old you are
abnormally quiet.

Bertha looks down at the word "abnormal".

Charlie (*cont'd*)
I mean, *unusually* quiet…I haven't said
anything wrong, have I? I mean nothing to
offend you in any way, shape, form or size?
(*Bertha shakes her head "no".*) Or color? Or
texture? Or luminosity?

Bertha
Luminosity?

Charlie
(*Amazed that she has spoken.*) Yes, luminosity.
You know… (*He gives dictionary definition.*)
"…containing a certain quantity of light,

illumination or iridescence… the quality of
glowing…sparkling, or shimmering… radiant, '
shining, aflame, afire…"

Bertha
No.

Charlie
(*Not understanding.*) No?

Bertha
No. You haven't offended me.

Charlie
Oh (*Pauses.*) Really? Not at all?

Bertha
(*Not able to look at him.*) Not at all.

Charlie
Sure?

Bertha
Yes!

Charlie
Good, then I'll continue. So…as to the subject
of the tuna fish, another reason not to eat them
is that some say the method of their capture
has been highly illicit, immoral, shameful,
even illegal perhaps, what with the growing
number of dolphins getting caught in the traps
and becoming extinct in the process –

Bertha

Who are you??

Charlie

Charlie. I'm Charlie. And you're Bertha.

Bertha

You know my name?

Charlie

We've known each other for weeks.

Bertha

We have?

Charlie

Yes. In my mind, in the dark recesses of my mind, I've been talking to you for weeks and we've become very good friends by now.

Bertha

During recess?

Charlie

Not recess, *recesses*…dark *places* in my mind, hidden places, areas of fantasy or daydreams…

Bertha

(*Feeling nervous.*) Oh. You've got a very large vocabulary.

Charlie

I've been working very hard on it, thank you.

I read the dictionary every night. Webster's, Third Edition.

Bertha
Oh.

Charlie
I take it you're not familiar with Webster's?

Bertha
Not very.

Charlie
It's not very exciting. It has no plot.

Bertha
How come you read it then?

Charlie
I'm accumulating words.

Bertha
Oh.

Charlie
Oh yourself.

Bertha
What kind of words?

Charlie
Magical ones. Distraught ones. Ancient ones. Poetic ones. Ones to describe the beautiful things I see, places, even people…who are beautiful, and therefore require description.

Bertha stares at him in complete shock.

Charlie (cont'd)

(*Loud voice.*)   Earth to Bertha, do you read me?
(*He shakes her lightly.*)   You're looking at me like
I'm some kind of an alien.

Bertha

You're new at this school.

Charlie

Yup.   Very new.   So new, you could even say
this was my first day.

Bertha

Who told you my name?

Charlie

I told you, *you* did…in one of our previous
conversations.

Bertha

What previous conversations???

Charlie

Don't hurt my feelings, Bertha.

Bertha

What did we talk about?

Charlie

All about your wooden leg.

Bertha

What???

Charlie

Your wooden leg. How you spent the good portion of your childhood in Hawaii. How you're planning to join The Merchant Marines after 6th grade is over. Why you pour whiskey in your chocolate milk.

Bertha

You're crazy.

Charlie

Yup.

Bertha

I have to leave now.

Charlie

Oh, come on, Bertha…I was just kidding you.

Bertha

You were?

Charlie

Yes.

Bertha

Oh. So who told you my name?

Charlie

Honest?

Bertha

Honest.

Charlie
Truth?

Bertha
Truth!

Charlie
George Washington.

Bertha
Who?

Charlie
I'm sorry, I meant The National Guard.

Bertha
What?

Charlie
Excuse me, my mistake again…I seem to be having difficulty concentrating today…Did I say the National Guard?

Bertha
Yes…

Charlie
Seems to be one of my off days, what I meant to say was…Tiny Simko told me your name. I asked her, and she told me your name.

Bertha
Oh. (*She looks down.*)

Charlie

Something the matter? (*He looks at her for a moment. She says nothing.*) You're sort of a …quiet type, right? No, no, let me guess…I'll bet you're…*shy.* (*Pause.*) You okay in there? (*Bertha nods.*) Sure?

Bertha

(*Nodding again.*) Yes.

They pause for a moment.

Charlie

Bertha.

Bertha

What?

Charlie

What are you thinking about?

Bertha

Luminosity.

Charlie

Oh. You like that word?

Bertha

(*Shrugs.*) I think so.

Charlie

It suits you. (*Pause. Bertha is silent, not quite sure what to make of that.*) It's a good word, a very good word. There's others, many others you might like as well…maybe you'd like to

hear some more tomorrow…at lunch
again…that is, if you're not previously
engaged.

Bertha
Previously engaged?

Charlie
Yes, if you're available.

Bertha
I guess.

Charlie
Okay…good. Um…Bertha…I gotta go back to
class in a little bit but…um…if my Mom or
Dad asks me if I made any new friends today,
can I just say that I made one real nice
one…and her name is Bertha? Just so they
don't think I bombed out on my first day or
anything, and spent it all alone…Can you do
me that one favor?

Bertha
Okay.

Charlie
Just 'cause I don't want them to worry about
me or anything, you know.

Bertha
Okay.

They sit for a few moments in silence, a little awkwardly.

Bertha *(cont'd)*

Why accumulating words?

Charlie

(Relieved to be off the other subject, quickly.) Well,
you know…words can come in very handy,
you know. Sometimes. For certain occasions.
You know?

Bertha

Oh. *(Pause.)* No.

Charlie

Well…for example, like…for days like today.
When you want to meet somebody
who…you've never met before…who you
would like to meet… Words are one way that
you can do that. *(He leans into her ear.)* Capiche?

Bertha

(Thinking he's sneezed.) Guzunteit.

Charlie

Hey, you speak a little German there, too,
Bertha! That's terrific…I mean really terrific.
I'm a quarter Italian myself, but, uh,
anyway…well, we can talk more about it later
sometime, Bertha, okay? Like maybe
tomorrow at lunch, alright? Okay?

Bertha

Okay.

Bell rings. Charlie gets up.

Charlie
See you later, Bertha. See you 'round.

Bertha
Bye, Charlie…

Charlie leaves.

Bertha (*cont'd*)
…See you 'round.

S C E N E   T W O :
"VOYAGES"

The next day. Bertha is eating lunch and Charlie is reading Webster's Dictionary.

Bertha
Charlie?

Charlie
What?

Bertha
What did we talk about?

Charlie
When?

Bertha
All those weeks…before you knew me.

Charlie

Oh, *then.* Well, um…we talked about many
things…many, many things…for instance…
about your long journey…overseas.

Bertha

Where overseas?

Charlie

(*Thinking.*) Well, to several places…
Indonesia…Bali…but mostly to a certain
tropical rain forest South of Fiji. There, you
only ate derelict penguins shipped from the
Northernmost territories of the Antarctic.

Bertha

Why only penguins? Penguins are cute.

Charlie

Yes, I know. But these were derelict
penguins…trouble-makers. Broke all sorts of
penguin rules and were a menace to penguin
society at large.

Bertha

(*Not believing him.*) I never heard of that,
Charlie.

Charlie

Watch *Wild Kingdom* sometime.

Bertha

I *do* watch *Wild Kingdom.*

Charlie

(Ignoring her.) In the rain forest, see, you need
a certain amount of a very special protein in
order to survive… And it's only found in
penguin meat…in a certain special chemical
that's been built up in their bones over
centuries of time —

Bertha
Why did it build up in their bones?

Charlie
Well...from having lived for so long in the Arctic, so far North and...under such harsh conditions. Special chemicals always build up that way.

Bertha
Yeah?

Charlie
Yeah.

Bertha
That's the way special things build up? Under harsh conditions?

Charlie
Yes, under very harsh conditions... During hardships.

Bertha
Oh. (*Pause.*) This story isn't true.

Charlie
(*Getting frustrated.*) Bertha, you wanted to know what we talked about in our previous conversations, and you asked me to tell you so I think the least you can do is listen and think about it! Especially since you're the one having trouble remembering!

Bertha

It's not my fault I can't remember!

Charlie

You just don't *want* to remember. It's laziness.

Bertha

It's not laziness, Charlie! It's that you're
insane! You make up these stories in your
head and then when I don't know about them,
I'm supposed to be stupid! That's not fair,
Charlie! That's not very nice! You're just
crazy, and I don't want to be your friend
anymore if you're going to treat me like that!

Charlie

Bertha, you're missing the whole point!

Bertha

What point?

Charlie

About the penguins, see —

Bertha

Charlie!

Charlie

What?

Bertha

You can't just go back to talking about the
penguins now!

Charlie
Why not?

Bertha
Because I'm fighting with you!

Charlie
(*Matter-of-factly.*) We're not fighting, Bertha. You're having a memory problem, and I'm straightening you out.

Bertha
Right, Charlie. I'm leaving. You're really out of control!

Charlie
Bertha! Wait!

Bertha
No!

Charlie
Okay, so maybe we didn't talk about this stuff...Maybe we didn't talk about it at all. We talked about other stuff, okay?

Bertha
Like what?

Charlie
Like...about why you eat alone on the playground every day...even though you're actually the most *popular* girl in school...

Bertha
(*Shocked.*) We did? We said that?

Charlie
Yes, you told me that you *chose* to eat alone, because...(*Making it up as he goes.*) ...no one here is really smart enough to carry on a conversation at the level of intelligence that you require.

Bertha
(*Amazed.*) Really? ...And...what else...did I say?

Charlie
Oh, lots of things...that you had lived all over the world, in a hundred different cities...and you spoke a hundred different languages. Including Indonesian. And so nothing new ever scared you. You were never afraid to be new or to meet anyone new.

Bertha
Charlie. This story isn't true, either.

Charlie
Sure it's true. There's a whole realm of possibility out there. You could become anything. You could become anything you want to.

(*Bertha stares at Charlie dumbfounded.*)

Charlie (cont'd)
You just have to keep seeing what you want in

your mind's eye. Keep seeing it, keep seeing it
there. And ask your spirit guides for help, or
something like that. (*Bertha continues to stare.*)
Hey, don't look at me. *I* didn't make it up. I
read it in one of my Mom's self-help books.
I'm pretty sure it works, though. It worked for
my Mom. That's how she got her dream job.
She used to work for lawyers – now she's
produce manager at Zabar's.

Bertha
Wow.

Charlie
I know. She's much happier now. Those
lawyers practically killed her. Now she gets to
arrange apples and oranges all day. Plus we're
eating a lot more fruits and vegetables. It's a
much better deal all around.

Bertha
My mom saw stuff in her mind's eye. All the
time.

Charlie
What do you mean?

Bertha
She just saw stuff. Invisible things. Gnomes.
Fairies. Magic people.

Charlie
Could you?

Bertha

No, but when she was around, I had a feeling that they were around, too. Now that she's gone, I don't think they know where to find me.

Charlie

Do you think she saw her spirit guides?

Bertha

She saw everything. But finally, all the invisible things just took her away.

Charlie

They took her away?

Bertha

She said she'd rather be with them than at home. (*She pauses.*) She said that if you were very, very quiet, you could hear them. You had to be really quiet, though, and wait to hear them. Wait and wait and wait.

Charlie

Bertha. Is that why you're so quiet? 'Cause you're waiting?

Bertha

Maybe.

Charlie

Well…have you seen them yet?

Bertha

Nope. I'm still waiting. Waiting for a little

magic. (*Charlie just looks at her.*) I know when they come and find me, it will be like my mom is back again. Like things are magical. And nothing is bad.

Charlie
You should travel in your mind. Bad things don't happen there.

Bertha
They don't?

Charlie
Not if you don't want them to.

A moment. Bertha takes this in.

Bertha
Charlie. Is that why you talk all the time? About sailing to places like Indonesia?

Charlie
Maybe.

Bertha
I see. (*Pause.*) So…what were you telling me about those penguins?

Charlie
Huh?

Bertha
The penguins…you know…the penguins in Indonesia? Or wherever it was?

Charlie

Oh. Oh yeah. (*Clears throat.*) …yes, of course, the penguins…uh, well, as I was saying..

Bertha

Yes?

Charlie

Well…we spoke at great length all about your travels to Indo-china and then to the South Pacific…

Bertha

Uh huh…

Charlie

…all about how you crossed the Pacific ocean accompanied only by moonlight in a birch-bark canoe…and then you were ship-wrecked —

Bertha

(*Alarmed.*) I was ship-wrecked?

Charlie

— on your way to Bora-Bora, but you were miraculously saved by a strange tribe of cannibals —

Bertha

(*Alarmed again.*) Cannibals???

Charlie

(*Sensing her alarm.*) — who decided *not* to eat you –

The lights begin to change and grow dim.

> ### Bertha
> Why didn't they eat me?

> ### Charlie
> Too skinny.

> ### Bertha
> I am???

> ### Charlie
> Okay, because you were too fat —

> ### Bertha
> Charlie!

> ### Charlie
> Well, what do you want? Okay, they wouldn't eat a kid with glasses, that's why. Like you shouldn't hit someone with glasses.

> ### Bertha
> You shouldn't?

> ### Charlie
> No, haven't you ever heard that?

Pink, a frantically paranoid girl enters. She is looking around as if someone is after her. Pink's style of clothing and jewelry is wild, fantastical and funky. (Please see costume notes on page 135.)

S C E N E   T H R E E :
"PINK"

Pink
(*To Bertha.*) You haven't seen any gypsies around here, have you?

Bertha
Gypsies?

Pink
Yeah, gypsies! Gypsies! Don't you know what gypsies are?

Bertha
Well, I, uh—

Pink
Well, have you or haven't you?

Bertha
Well, I don't think so.

Pink
What do you mean you don't think so? Have you or haven't you? This is important!

Charlie
Who wants to know?

Pink
Pink.

Charlie
What's pink?

Pink
I'm Pink.

Charlie
You don't look pink.

Pink
No, no…my *name*.   My *name* is *Pink*.

Charlie
Your name is Pink?

Pink
Yesseree, Bob.

Charlie
No. I'm Charlie. My name is Charlie, and this here is Bertha.

Pink
Pleased to make your acquaintance. So have you seen any gypsies, or haven't you?

Charlie
Well, Pink, it just so happens you're looking at one.

Bertha
Charlie, I didn't know you were a gypsy!

Charlie
Just a quarter on my mother's side. We don't talk about it much.

Bertha
Why are you looking for gypsies, Pink?

Pink
I'm not looking for them. They're looking for me. I can't really talk now. I just got here. Drove all the way in my father's Cadillac. Do you know what that does to your *back?*

Bertha
You drove a car?

Pink
'67 Caddy. It's a sight to see.

Bertha
Your Dad lets you drive?

Pink
My Dad doesn't let me do anything. I stole the dang car.

Bertha
You stole it?

Pink
Well, of course I stole it. How do you think you get anything in this life?

Charlie
How can you see over the dashboard?

Pink
I sit on a couple of phone books. The Texas phone book is really fat, you know.

Charlie
So you drove from *Texas?*

Pink
Just south of the border. My Dad's a gambler.

Charlie
Gambles in Mexico, eh?

Pink
In Rio, to be precise. Look, my eyes are sore, I've got a terrible sunburn, my fingers are blistered from clutching the wheel...do you mind if I sit down?

Bertha

How could you leave your Dad behind?

Pink

I couldn't help it. The Feds got him. Locked
him up and threw away the key. Truthfully
speaking, it's a bad situation. A very bad, bad
situation. I can't even talk about it. I had to
sneak through immigration. Wore a pair of
dark sunglasses and a Groucho Marx disguise.
Used sign language and pretended to be deaf.
It was terrifying, simply terrifying. This is the
first stop I've made since I crossed the border.
I figured I could sneak into this school and get
a hot lunch.

Bertha

You ate hot lunch?

Pink

First thing I've eaten in days. I was afraid to
stop. There's a warrant out for my arrest. The
gypsies own me.

Bertha

(*Enthralled.*) The gypsies own you?

Pink

Yeah, my Dad gave me away to them as
collateral when one of his deals went bust. Sold
me to be some magician's assistant. I couldn't
stand it. Getting cut in half all day. Standing on
stage in a tutu with a big grin plastered on my
face. I ran away a hundred times. Whenever
they caught me, they stuck cactus needles in my

hands and feet.... You have any idea, what that feels like, all those thorns? I packed it up. Hot-wired the Caddy. Now I'm here. You have to be daring or you die.

Charlie
So...you're on the lam.

Pink
That's right, Buster. So, have you seen 'em, or not?

Bertha
Who?

Pink
(*Exploding.*) The gypsies, the gypsies goddammit! I've gotta shake 'em this time! I can't take much more! My wild days are over!

Charlie
Why don't you stay a while?

Bertha
Put your feet up.

Charlie
Take a load off.

Bertha
Hang your hat up.

Pause.

Charlie
It's a figure of speech.

Pink
(*Sitting down next to them.*) If you insist.

S C E N E   F O U R :
"GYPSY SPELL"

Bertha
We insist.

Charlie
Where are you staying, Pink?

Pink
I just live in the Cadillac. But once in a while I splurge and stay at Motel 6.

Bertha
But how do you get money for that?

Pink
I make jewelry out of dried fruits and raisins and sell it by the side of the road. And once in a while I get a gig doing a manicure.

Bertha
You do manicures? How did you learn to do that?

Pink

Anyone can put polish on a fingernail. It's a
big scam. No one should ever pay anyone to
polish their nails. (*Pause.*) I also tell fortunes.

Bertha

Maybe we should hide you somewhere.

Pink

Hide me from the gypsies?

Charlie

What about the Cadillac?

Pink

Don't worry about it. It's safely parked in a
driveway. I just hope the gypsies don't
recognize it. I can barely think about my days
with the gypsies. Too painful. Terrible. You
can't begin to imagine.

*Pink pulls out a hanky and cries dramatically. Charlie and
Bertha try to comfort her.*

Bertha

Pink, Pink, please…! (*Pink cries harder.*)
Pink…! Pink, please…please don't cry. (*Pink
stops crying as abruptly as she started and wipes
her tears with the hanky.*) Are you okay?

Pink nods, still intense with emotion.

Charlie

We were worried about you for a minute there.

Pink

(*Barely able to compose herself.*) Thank you.
Thank you for your kindness.

Charlie

Man.

Bertha

Man.

Charlie

We have to do something about those gypsies.
They're tearing you apart.

Bertha

I agree.

Pink

Could you?

Charlie

We have to.

Bertha

But what could we do?

Charlie

We could fight them on the information
superhighway. Use computers.

Pink

Gypsies don't have computers. They travel
too much.

Charlie

Not even laptops?

Pink

Nope. They don't even have typewriters or
pencils. Everything's passed on through
stories and drawings. And magic spells.

Charlie

That's it!

Pink

What's it?

Charlie

That's how we'll get to those gypsies! We'll
cast a magic spell.

Pink

But I don't know any magic spells.

Charlie

Not even from when you were a magician's
assistant?

Pink

Naw. I was more of an ornament than
anything else.

Charlie

Hmph.

Pause.

Bertha
I believe *I* can remember a spell or two.

Charlie & Pink
You do?

Bertha
Yes. One I learned when I lived in Indonesia.
When I was in total isolation. A Polynesian
wind spirit taught me how.

Pink
You've got to cast it now! Before they get here
and find me.

Bertha
Okay, hold on. I have to remember.

Pink
Hurry. I can sense the gypsies on their way. It
won't be too long now. I can feel it.

Bertha
Don't panic. Just give me a moment.

*Bertha closes her eyes and puts her hands over her head and
tilts her head back. A moment or two passes like that.*

Pink
What is she doing?

Charlie
She's concentrating.

*Bertha mumbles something inaudible with her eyes still
closed.*

Pink

What is she saying?

Charlie

(*Making it up.*) She's...invoking the Polynesian spirit guides.

Bertha continues to mumble, opens her arms wide.

Pink

What's she doing now?

Charlie

I...believe she's receiving guidance from the wind.

Bertha makes a loud high pitched sound.

Pink

Now what? Now what?

Charlie

I think we're supposed to howl, too.

Charlie and Pink begin to howl with Bertha. This continues for some time. They move in a kind of dance, getting louder and louder.

Bertha

(*Suddenly.*) All freeze!

They all freeze.

Bertha (*cont'd*)

They're here!

Charlie

Prepare for battle!

They run frantically in different directions into hiding places. Tiny enters, still holding her basketball. She is small physically, but her presence is enormous. She is feisty, but she means well.

Tiny

What the hell is going on here?

Charlie

Tiny!

Tiny

Mrs. Markowitz told me to tell you guys to keep it down over here. She's in a rotten mood. There's an unidentified Cadillac blocking the driveway so she couldn't make her lunch date.

Charlie

(*To Pink.*) You parked in the school driveway?

Tiny

(*Recognizing Pink.*) Hey! Didn't you come to my house the other day and do my Mom's nails?

Charlie

(*To Tiny.*) You know Pink?

Pink

We've met.

Tiny
My Mom's nails all broke and the polish peeled off. She said she wants a refund.

Pink
I can't help it if your Mom isn't delicate with her hands.

Charlie
Dammit, Tiny, we're in the middle of something important here and you're throwing the whole thing off. *I'll* re-do your mother's nails personally if you'll just beat it.

Tiny
Well, whatever it is you were doing, keep the volume down. Or you're all going to the principal's office.

Tiny exits. A moment. They all look around.

Charlie
It worked.

Pink
How do you know?

Charlie
Do you see any gypsies? Besides me, I mean.

Pink
I can't say I do.

Bertha
(*To Pink.*) What will you do now? Now that you're out of danger?

Pink

I guess I should go back and rescue my Dad.
The Feds locked him up and threw away the
key. I just can't leave him to rot in that jail cell.

Bertha

Yeah.

Charlie

Yeah.

Pink

It'll be hard.

Charlie

Can you put it off?

Pink

Not really. I should go. Besides, my car is
blocking the school driveway. Your teacher
will never get married if she can't go out on
her lunch dates.

Bertha

I suppose you have a point. But Pink, be
careful.

Pink

I will.

Charlie

You know where we are in case you ever need
to find us.

Pink

That's true. I'll always know where to find you.

Pink exits. Charlie and Bertha watch her go.

Bertha

(*Excited.*) Charlie. I feel like my Mom is back. I feel like I did when she was alive.

Charlie

What do you mean?

Bertha

It's Pink. Pink's magic. There's magic in the air.

Charlie

You think she's magic?

Bertha

She has to be. I feel totally different. Do you think she'll ever come back?

Charlie

I don't know. I hope so.

Bertha

Let's be quiet and wait.

Charlie

We have to be totally quiet? Totally?

Bertha

That's what my mother said, Charlie. That's the way it's done.

Charlie

I don't know if I can do that.

Bertha

Try, Charlie.

Charlie

Okay.

They sit with their eyes closed, very quietly, without moving. Lights change.

S C E N E   F I V E :
"BREAKDOWN"

Moments later. Charlie and Bertha still sit in silence. Pink enters, hastily, and out of breath.

Pink

Hello, sportsfans.

Bertha

Pink! What are you doing back?

Pink

Car broke down fifty miles outside of Toluca Lake. I was afraid to go on without my wheels so I hitched a ride back here. I'll have to try again tomorrow. Get a good night's rest and start fresh.

Charlie looks at his watch.

Bertha
But what about your Dad?

Pink
I can't stand to think of him wasting away in that jail cell. But with my car in the shop I have no other choice but to wait. It's too risky to make the trip without the green bomber.

Charlie
Keep the faith, Pink. Don't give up.

Pink
Never.

Pink salutes, runs off, leaving Bertha and Charlie staring after her, wide-eyed.

Bertha
She is –

Charlie
She is –

Bertha
She's magic –

Charlie
She is –

Bertha
Oh my God –

Charlie
She could never drive all that way –

Bertha
– and then drive all the way back –

Charlie
– unless she flew –

Bertha
– maybe she flew –

Charlie
She's magic. Definitely magic.

Bertha
Pink's magic.

Pink re-enters, carrying an over-night bag.

Pink
Don't tell anyone, but in this bag I have two
million dollars worth of solid gold. Bribe
money for the jail guards when I get to Rio.

*The Woman enters. She carries a purse and car keys, and is
in a hurry.*

Woman
(*To Pink.*) Come on Nancy, let's go. Oh, good,
you found your bag.

*A horrible moment. Charlie and Bertha stare at Pink. Pink
stares at The Woman. The Woman stares at Pink. Charlie
and Bertha stare at The Woman.*

Woman (*cont'd*)
(*To Pink.*) I hope you packed everything
you're gonna need, 'cause I don't have time to
stop back at home, Nance.

Pink
(*To Charlie and Bertha.*) If I don't surrender
now, it'll just be worse later. I've been through
this before.

Woman
Nance, let's go. I've got the car blocking the
driveway and no one can get by.

Pink
(*Resigned.*) They finally got me.

Woman
It took me forever to find you. No one at this
school seems to know who you are! (*She puts
her arm around Pink and starts to lead her away.*)

Charlie leaps up and tackles The Woman to the ground.

Woman (*cont'd*)
Oh, my God…! Cut that out! Stop it!!!

Charlie
(*As he wrestles with The Woman.*) Run, Pink!
Run while you still have the chance!

Bertha grabs Pink by the hand and runs off with her.

Charlie (*cont'd*)
(*Pinning The Woman to the ground.*) I see

through you! I know what you're doing!
Posing as Pink's mother…! Pink doesn't even
have a mother! She does manicures for a
living! She drives a Cadillac! She sells dried
raisins by the side of the road! You've no right
to even *say* you're her mother! I've never
heard her even *mention* she had a mother!

Woman
GET OFF OF ME!!!

Charlie
Impostor! Charlatan! Fraud! Rogue! Ruffian!

The Woman finally manages to throw Charlie off.

Woman
Are you totally out of your mind!!! What the
hell do you think you're doing?

Charlie
Don't make another move.

Woman
What is going on here?!? This is insane!

Charlie paces around her, keeping her trapped in one spot.

Woman (cont'd)
Please. (*She is visibly upset.*) Oh, my God. This
is too much. This is not happening. I want to
know your name.

Charlie
Charlie. I'm Charlie. And you're the gypsy queen.

Woman
Uh, huh. Well, Charlie, if I'm the gypsy *queen,* would you mind telling me where you think the gypsy *princess* went? 'Cause I've got twenty more gypsy *minutes* to get back to the gypsy *salon* and cut four more heads of gypsy *hair.* And I don't want to lose my gypsy *job.* You understand?

Charlie
Good alibi.

Woman
Okay, kid, where'd she go?

Charlie
I'll never tell. She's on the lam.

Woman
You can't be for real.

The Woman makes a move but Charlie blocks her way.

Charlie
You're not going anywhere.

Woman
(*Sighs.*) I'll tell you what I'm gonna do.

Charlie
I should let you know right now…I can't be bought.

Woman
Well, that's good to know, 'cause I couldn't

pay you very much anyway. (*She fluffs her hair back in place a little, an attempt to regain what's left of her dignity.*) Just give Nancy the following message, will you?

Charlie
If you keep the code words to a minimum.

Woman
Tell her I'm going to get my car out of the school driveway. I'm going to double park it out front by the crosswalk. And I'm going to wait five, maybe six minutes, tops. If I don't see her in the car by then, she will *not* be able to go to her Dad's for the weekend. 'Cause I really don't have time for this.

Charlie
She'll be in Rio for the weekend. She's gotta rescue him from the Feds.

Woman
Who?

Charlie
The Feds.

Woman
No, *who?*

Charlie
Oh. Her Dad, of course. They locked him up and threw away the key.

The Woman seems tired all of a sudden.

Woman

Well. I...just. Just tell her. Tell her we can talk about it in the car.

The Woman exits. Charlie stands there, watching her go.

S C E N E   S I X :
"TRANSFORMATION"

Another area of the play ground. Pink and Bertha are crouched in hiding.

Bertha

I guess my spell didn't work.

Pink

It was a good try. (*Pause.*) Want to wear some of my beads?

Bertha

Okay.

Pink takes one strand of many beads from around her neck and puts them on Bertha.

Pink

Hey, you look pretty good in those. Here. Take some more. (*She steps back and looks at Bertha for a moment.*) Hey, I just got an idea. (*She grabs her bag and rummages through it, pulls out powder and rouge.*)

Bertha

What are you doing?

Pink dabs Bertha with powder and rouge.

Bertha

Pink, you're crazy!

Pink

Hold still. (*She grabs a lipstick.*) Open wide. (*She applies lipstick to Bertha.*) Red is definitely your color. (*She hands Bertha a tissue.*) Now blot.

Bertha

Red's my color?

Pink

Sure looks that way.

Pink takes Bertha's hair out of it's pony tail and brushes it.

Bertha

What's yours?

Pink

What do you think?

Bertha & Pink

…Pink!

Pink

(*Digging through her bag.*) And now, for the final touch… (*She produces an exotic flower hair clip, and clips it in Bertha's hair.*) …Voila! (*She hands a mirror to Bertha.*) Well, what do you think?

Bertha

Wow.

Pink

Incredible, huh?

Bertha

Oh, wow…

Pink

You look great. Let's go show Charlie!

Bertha

Pink, no…

Pink

Why not?

Bertha

Well…what if Charlie doesn't like me this way?

Pink

Why wouldn't he?

Bertha

I don't know. What he last saw me I was a completely different person.

Pink

So?

Bertha

He might not even recognize me!

Pink

That would be wild!

Pink grabs Bertha's hand, pulling her.

Bertha

Pink, wait! Pink, please! Let's wait! PINK!

Pink

What?

Bertha

What about the gypsy?

Pink

What gypsy?

Bertha

The gypsy who Charlie captured. Or who captured Charlie.

Pink

Oh, her. She's probably gone by now.

Lights fade as Pink pulls Bertha off-stage.

Bertha

(*From off-stage.*) No...Pink! No!

S C E N E   S E V E N :
"RESPLENDENCE"

Several minutes later. Charlie sits alone, a little despondent. Pink rushes in, dragging Bertha by the hand.

Pink

Well?

Bertha

Well?

Charlie

Well? (*Noticing Bertha.*) Oh, my God.

Bertha

(*Covering her face.*) Oh, no...

Pink
(*To Charlie.*) What do you think?

Charlie
Bertha? (*To Pink.*) That's Bertha, right?

Pink
That's her.

Charlie
Bertha...you look... (*Bertha peeks out at Charlie.*)
...resplendent.

Pink
(*To Bertha.*) Is that good?

Bertha
(*Grabbing Charlie's dictionary.*) I'm not sure.
Let me check. (*Reads.*) ... "radiant, bright,
shining, shiny, brilliant..."

Pink
(*Still not sure.*) So he likes it, right?

Bertha
Thanks, Charlie. That's real sweet of you.

Pink
(*Relieved.*) He likes it.

Bertha
Charlie, if it weren't for Pink, I wouldn't know
that red is my color.

Charlie
Red is your color?

Bertha
(*Strikes a glamorous pose.*) Sure looks that way!

The bell rings. They gather their books and bags.

Bertha
(*Touching the beads around her neck.*) Pink! You better take these back!

Pink
Keep them. I have a hundred others at home.

Bertha
Sure?

Pink
Sure! (*Pink starts to exit.*)

Bertha
Thanks, Pink!

Charlie
(*Remembering.*) Oh, Pink!

Pink
What?

Charlie
Where are you going?

Pink
To Rio!

Charlie
Pink...I think there's an *express* flight to Rio. You might want to catch it.

Pink
What time?

Charlie
In the next two minutes. It leaves from the front entrance to the school. Right by the crosswalk. But you have to hurry or you'll miss it.

Pink
Is it a helicopter or just a regular plane?

Charlie
It's...it's a rocket ship.

Pink
Oh, my God! I don't have a thing to wear!

Charlie
(*Motions for her to go.*) Pink, it's leaving! It's leaving right now!

Pink
I'll send you a postcard! (*Runs off, then turns back, salutes.*) To Rio!

Pink exits. Charlie and Bertha look at one another. There is an awkward moment.

Bertha
Well...see you tomorrow, Charlie.

Charlie

Okay.

They start walking in different directions.

Charlie (*cont'd*)

Hey, Bertha?

Bertha

Yeah, Charlie?

Charlie

Did I mention that you look...radiant, superb, artistic, exquisite, bewitching, enchanting, fetching and dazzling?

Bertha

(*Embarrassed.*) Thanks, Charlie.

Charlie

You're welcome.

Bertha

Thanks for the words.

Charlie

You know how I feel about words.

Blackout.

S C E N E   E I G H T:
"THOUGHTS OF RIO"

Several days later. Lights up on Charlie and Bertha. Charlie pages through the dictionary. Bertha fingers her beads absent-mindedly. She still wears the big hair clip that Pink gave her, and her hair is still loose the way Pink did it.

Bertha
Do you ever wonder about Pink?

Charlie
Do you?

Bertha
I feel bad about Pink.

Charlie
Pink can handle herself. She's magic.

Bertha
What if she's in danger, Charlie?

Pause.

Charlie
Rio *is* a rough town.

Pause.

Bertha
Should I try to find her?

Charlie
If you want.

Bertha exits.

S C E N E   N I N E :
"TROUBLE AT THE BORDER"

---

*The same day. Another section of the playground. Pink is
alone playing jacks. She uses raisins, jewelry and other
strange assorted items as jacks. Bertha enters.*

Bertha
Pink! How was Rio? Did you find your Dad?

Pink gives no response.

Bertha (*cont'd*)
Well, did you?

Pink
I found him all right.

Bertha
Well, what happened? Did you get him out of
jail?

Pink
I got him out of jail. But he couldn't cross the
border.

Bertha

Why not?

Pink

He didn't have all the right paperwork. He's no longer allowed in America.

Bertha

Oh, Pink...I'm sorry.

Pink

(*Fighting tears.*) It's no biggie. He says he likes it there fine. The hot sun and the dancing girls... (*She can't speak anymore.*)

Bertha

Oh, Pink.

They sit together in silence. Tears well up. A few moments go by.

Bertha

Charlie misses you.

Pink

He does? Is he still reading the dictionary?

Bertha

Yup. He knows a ton of words now. He knows so many words, he talks all the time, just so he can use them all.

Pink

Does he tell stories?

Bertha
Non-stop.

Pink
Non-stop stories?

Bertha
He's a walking, talking, non-stop story-teller.
He's just full of words. They're like
explosions. Words just keep exploding out of
him all the time.

Pink
I suppose that's what happens when you
know so many words. If you don't talk all the
time, you won't get to say them all.

Bertha
That's Charlie.

They stand up to go. Pink gathers her things.

Pink
You won't tell him about my Dad, will you?

Bertha
No problem.

Pink
'Cause I don't want him to know that I couldn't save him, you know.

Bertha
No problem.

S C E N E   T E N :
"STARS"

A few days later. Bertha, Charlie and Pink are onstage. Charlie has been telling a story in which Bertha and Pink are the stars, and they listen to him, entranced.

Charlie
So then you flew up to the moon on a magic horse…

Bertha
Yeah…?

Pink

We did...?

Charlie

...and you were flying in circles, and these
stars landed in your hair...

Bertha

There were stars in our hair?

Charlie

...a million little stars just tumbled out of the
stratosphere and fell into your hair...and you
reached out to grab some more and they just
kept falling, falling like snow...falling from
out of nowhere...and they kept falling until
you were both totally covered with these
minuscule but very shiny, brilliant little stars...

Bertha

How big were they?

Charlie

About the size of a lady bug.

Pink

That's small all right. In astronomy, Miss
Willis said that stars are huge, like planets.

Charlie

Well, these were very small stars. Tiny, in fact.
And they fell and they fell and they kept on
falling until finally you were both covered

with zillions of glimmering, dazzling, radiant stars, all over your arms and your faces…and all the other stars started to circle you, and they formed constellations around you, and you were able to jump off the horse and fly on your own from star to star…doing somersaults in the air…and back-flips…

Bertha
But Charlie…were *you* there?

Charlie
…and I was there and I was doing handstands on the stars and all the Martians were placing bets on which one of us would fly the highest, but it didn't matter 'cause we all held hands and kept taking each other higher and higher …until there was no where left to go. So we landed on the moon and watched the stars explode like fireworks in the sky, like a fourth of July extravaganza that would never, ever end…

Silence. A few moments go by. They are all caught up in a reverie.

Pink
And then what happened?

Bertha
Yeah, then what happened?

Charlie
Well, I don't know. I think we're still up there.

Pink
We're up there right now?

Charlie
That's how it feels. As far as I know, we're still there.

Pause. All three wait and wonder.

Pink
We're still up there, aren't we?

Bertha
I think so.

Charlie
I think so, too. (*He looks at both of them.*) You both still have stars in your hair.

He smiles. Pink and Bertha smile back. They all turn and continue to stare upwards.

Tiny walks by, in the darkness, bouncing her basketball. She doesn't seem to notice them at all.

Lights fade.

THE END

About the author...

Kerry Muir has taught acting to children and teens at The Lee Strasberg Theatre Institutes in New York and Los Angeles, Children of the Night, The Los Angeles Youth Network, and at Class Act's Young Actor's Studio. Her play *Befriending Bertha* won first prize in the 1995 Nantucket Short Play Festival and second prize in the 1995 Great Platte River Playwrights' Festival. Her work with young actors led her to publish an anthology of scenes and monologues for ages 7-14, *Childsplay* (Limelight Editions, 1995).